HAN... ...ER
MAT... ...AL

Analysing individual and team play is essential when improving performance in soccer, but identifying the right information and putting it to good use can be difficult. This is the first book to focus entirely on match analysis in the game of soccer.

Representing an essential and unique resource, this handbook looks at the very latest in match analysis research, and at the innovative technologies being used by professional clubs. Bridging the gap between theory and practice, it documents the methods by which coaches, sport scientists and fitness coaches can improve individual and team performance in soccer. The following areas are covered:

- tactics, technical ability and physical fitness
- how to supply objective feedback to players
- how to develop specific training routines
- manual, video and computerised match analysis systems
- current research findings in soccer match analysis

By combining the latest scientific data and methods of analysis with the practical advice needed by those on the sideline, this book breaks new ground and offers a clear glimpse into the future of match analysis.

Christopher Carling is a lecturer and consultant in match analysis. He is based at France's National Institute of Sport and Physical Education (INSEP) in Paris.

A. Mark Williams is Professor of Motor Behaviour at Liverpool John Moores University, UK. He has worked as a consultant to several professional clubs and National Federations.

Professor **Thomas Reilly** is Director of the research institute for Sport and Exercise Sciences at Liverpool John Moores University, UK and President of the World Commission of Science and Sports.

HANDBOOK OF SOCCER MATCH ANALYSIS

A SYSTEMATIC APPROACH TO IMPROVING
PERFORMANCE

Christopher Carling,
A. Mark Williams and Thomas Reilly

Routledge
Taylor & Francis Group

LONDON AND NEW YORK

First published 2005 by Routledge
2 Park Square, Milton Park, Abingdon, Oxon OX14 4RN

Simultaneously published in the USA and Canada
by Routledge
270 Madison Ave, New York, NY 10016

Reprinted 2007

Routledge is an imprint of the Taylor & Francis Group, an informa business

© 2005 Christopher Carling, A. Mark Williams and Thomas Reilly

Typeset in Bell Gothic by Keystroke, Jacaranda Lodge, Wolverhampton
Printed and bound in Great Britain by TJ International Ltd, Padstow, Cornwall

British Library Cataloguing in Publication Data
A catalogue record for this book is available from the British Library

Library of Congress Cataloging in Publication Data

Carling, Christopher, 1972–
Handbook of soccer match analysis / Christopher Carling, A. Mark Williams,
and Thomas P. Reilly.
   p. cm.
Includes bibliographical references and index.
ISBN 0–415–33908–1 (hardback) — ISBN 0–415–33909–X (pbk.) —
ISBN 0–203–44862–6 (ebook)
1. Soccer matches—Evaluation—Handbooks, manuals, etc.
2. Soccer—Training—Handbooks, manuals, etc.
3. Soccer—Ability testing—Handbooks, manuals, etc.
I. Williams, A. M. (A. Mark), 1965– II. Reilly, Thomas, 1941– III. Title.
GV943.9.T7C36 2005
796.334′64—dc22

                                                   2004029474

ISBN10: 0–415–33908–1 (hbk)
ISBN10: 0–415–33909–X (pbk)

ISBN13: 978–0–415–33908–7 (hbk)
ISBN13: 978–0–415–33909–4 (pbk)

▼ CONTENTS

▼ FIGURES

▼ TABLES

TABLES

▼ FOREWORD

The first manager I ever worked with in professional football used the *Rothman's Football Yearbook* for the information he needed about players, teams and track records. Primitive maybe, but he was a seeker of knowledge and often used the information as a catalyst for both team talks and buying players in the transfer market.

The first serious attempts to analyse the events and happenings in the game of football, to my knowledge, were conducted in the late 1940s and 1950s using a hand-notation system to compile the information. Match Analysis is now a fully accepted detection vehicle for any serious minded managerial and coaching staff but previously the science of Match Analysis had been spurned by many in football as being unnecessary and superfluous to the beautiful game. I would be extremely surprised if any Premiership Club and major international team did not now use Match Analysis in its quest for performance excellence and game results.

Staff at Liverpool John Moores University since my first contact with Tom Reilly in the 1980s and more recent involvement with Mark Williams, have always been at the forefront of research and especially research and investigation into the game of football. This book is testimony to the importance and significance of match analysis methods seen through the eyes of the authors and is for anyone seriously committed to the game of football. It provides students, sports scientists, coaches and managers with information, detail and insight into the game of football and advises all who read the book on the application of Match Analysis findings. The statement that 'coaches can only recall 50 per cent of the game events' (and I will add 'on a good day') indicates that for a comprehensive and detailed reflection on performance, a more precise and incisive method of 'knowing what happened' is essential in high level sports. Whether hand-notation, computerised video analysis or the more advanced and sophisticated Global Positioning System is utilised, a coach has a duty to himself, his players and his employer to be fully aware of the causes and facts behind performance.

From a brief history of Match Analysis to an appraisal of the differing systems, the book informs and educates us on the issues surrounding Match Analysis. The authors reveal significant technical and tactical findings with which coaches must be conversant. The physiological and athletic diagnosis of the game is also discussed and evaluated in a manner that all coaches can comprehend and imbibe.

In short, the book comprehensively and incisively advises readers on what is available, what we could analyse, how we could utilise the analysis findings, why we should analyse, what analysis can reveal and how we could devise practice, and relevant, meaningful practice at that, to benefit from our investment in the principle of Match Analysis.

It is a book that I have read with great interest both knowing the authors, for whom I have the greatest respect, and because of its sheer value in extending my knowledge and understanding of the game. Why all those interested in the game of football should read it, is crystallised in this statement in the book:

> 'successful coaches have an almost insatiable appetite for knowledge about every facet of the game'

I would advise all students of the game to invest in this book – it will make a significant contribution to their knowledge base and understanding of the mechanics of the game; it is essential reading for all coaches.

Dick Bate
FA National Coach

▼ FOREWORD

The analysis of performance is vital in soccer if the individual/team is to be successful. For many soccer coaches the information gained from performances will not only form the basis of weekly training programmes, but also may act as the primary source for the scheduling of seasonal plans.

In order to do this, and use performance analysis successfully, it is fundamental to have a clear strategy encompassing what you wish to analyse, how you are to undertake the process and most importantly how this information can then be translated and applied to benefit performance. Such details can often prove very difficult to determine as the 'what', 'how' and 'why' are often reliant on several factors that may affect the coach's choice one way or another.

Although match analysis is not new to sport, through developments in technology and the introduction of sport science to soccer it can be used in a number of different ways and a variety of formats. As coaches it is vital that we are aware of these developments to ensure that we are able to analyse performance in a contemporary way to improve individual and team play.

The *Handbook of Soccer Match Analysis* provides coaches with such information through an extensive introduction to the many ways of implementing performance analysis in soccer. Through the provision of soccer specific examples, contemporary statistics and discussions at several levels this handbook provides invaluable support to help coaches and sport scientists apply their findings in a practical setting to optimise player performance.

An ideal companion for all serious soccer coaches wishing to develop their knowledge of the processes of match analysis at the very highest level, this book successfully bridges the gap between theory and practice.

Kevin Thelwell
Director of Youth, Preston North End Football Club
Formerly Director of Coach Education, Football Association of Wales

▼ ACKNOWLEDGEMENTS

Many thanks to the companies Sport-Universal Process, ORAD, Sportscode, AVC Enterprises and Cairos, and to Mr Thierry Marszalek from the French Football Federation, for their contributions.

CHAPTER ONE

▼ INTRODUCTION TO SOCCER MATCH ANALYSIS

INTRODUCTION

Performance in ball games is much more difficult to appraise than it is in individual sports. In track-and-field athletics the competitor who passes the winning post first, jumps highest or longest, or throws the missile furthest becomes victorious. All competitors can be judged according to their finishing position, or on the time taken or distance achieved during performance. These kinds of metrics apply also to swimming, rowing, cycling, skiing and other events. In ball games the contest is decided by points or sets won, or goals scored. In soccer there is a simple determinant of victory: winning means scoring more goals than the opposition!

When a soccer team wins a game can rightly claim that the objective has been achieved. Thoughts can be refocused on moving on to the next game and securing another victory. There is, however, a distinction between the outcome (winning or losing) and the performance by which it was achieved. Since chance often plays a role in the scoring or conceding of goals – for example, an 'own goal' or a fluke deflection – coaches recognise that what they deemed to have been the better team does not always win the game. This kind of comment raises questions about what the basis for judging performance is and whether there are any clear criteria capable of being used as evidence.

It is only relatively recently that analytical techniques have been applied to competitive performance in field games. The traditional view was that these games were essentially an opportunity to display artistry and individual skills. Watching gifted players display their skills was an aesthetic experience, analogous to appreciating artistic performance in the theatre or music hall. The audience looks for elements of creativity when the player is in possession of the ball and appreciates flamboyant use of it in the context of performing. Those highlighted as 'flair players' get most adulation. It is not surprising that soccer has been dubbed 'the beautiful game'.

The disparate aspects of the game are evident in the historical origins of soccer. These are the emphasis on skill on the one hand and a focus on function on the other. Ball games have been traced back to ancient Chinese civilisation and the game of *tsh-chu*. The objective of the game was to propel a ball stuffed with feathers into a net suspended between two bamboo poles. This directed approach was contrasted with the more refined style adopted in Japanese culture. The activity was between two participants who attempted to keep the ball off the ground for as long as possible, using only their feet.

As soccer games spread through different civilisations, each promoting its own unique characteristics, they assumed either an entertainment or a participative function. The activity known as *calcio*, developed during the Renaissance in Italy, was an example of the former, whereas 'mob football' in Britain exemplified the latter. Entire villages participated in the mob version of the game, the object being to take the ball beyond a boundary point against the opponents' best attempts. Victory was achieved when the target point was reached. The number of marred and injured participants was irrelevant to the outcome, although individual consequences were sometimes grievous. The one thing that mattered publicly was that the game was won. It is likely that local acclaim was given to combatants at the centre of the brawling.

In the second half of the nineteenth century, the institutionalisation of soccer, first by the Football Association in England, brought order and rules of play to the chaotic versions of the game in preceding times. This formalisation was promoted by the public schools in England. Regulations were soon adopted in other European countries, and in other continents as the game developed worldwide. International matches increased in a tentative manner, as did the formalisation of the international governing body, FIFA (Fédération Internationale de Football Association), set up in 1904. The World Cup tournament first took place in 1930, meaning that the game only developed into a global competition following the First World War. A variety of styles of play became evident, which encouraged coaches to become more reflective and analytical about their own methods. The seeds of this extroversion were sown in the 1950s and 1960s, started to bloom in the 1970s and 1980s, and came to fruition in the 1990s. It is only in this past decade or so that formal match analysis has gained widespread acceptance among soccer coaches. Now, any coach who did not pursue performance analysis of some kind or other would be deemed negligent in the contemporary soccer community. Courses on match analysis are now routinely presented on coach education programmes around the world, and most professional clubs have access to match analysis in some form or other.

THE NATURE AND ORIGINS OF MATCH ANALYSIS

Match analysis refers to the objective recording and examination of behavioural events occurring during competition. It may be focused on the activity of one player, or may include the integration of actions and movements of players around the ball. Match analysis may range in sophistication from discrete data about the activity of an individual player, or of each member of the team as an individual profile, to a synthesis of the interplay between individuals in conformity to a team plan. Behaviour when defending and when attacking can be accommodated, as can the analysis of either one or both teams together. An outcome may be a description of the team's pattern of play.

Notational analysis

Notation analysis is essentially a means of recording events so that there is an accurate and objective record of what actually took place. Spectators view matches differently, often disagree about what happened and may be completely mistaken. Each individual brings his or her bias to the game and may see it from a partisan viewpoint. Even the best coaches are often unable to recall sequences of events correctly and fail to appreciate where successful plays originated or mistakes began. Notation analysis provides a factual record which does not lie – as long as the data collection methods used are reliable and objective and the system is adapted to the level of play.

The idea of notating human behaviour is historically well established. There is evidence that hieroglyphics were employed by the ancient Egyptians to record features of movement. The strategic deposition of military units has been used in warfare on both sea and land, and mapped out as plans of attack or defence. In more recent times a shorthand for analysing movements in dance, 'Laban notation', came into use. The tactic of using coded notes for analysing competitive performances was adopted by coaches in the United States of America, particularly in basketball and American football. The utility of the approach was soon recognised in the racket sports before it was more widely applied to soccer. Current systems are much more powerful and complex than early attempts to code activity in real time using manual or even audio-tape recordings. Contemporary uses go beyond the analysis of recent matches to the prediction and modelling of forthcoming contests. Styles of play and likely patterns of movement can be simulated either as physical models or as computer-driven virtual reality scenarios.

Prior to the evolution of computer-aided techniques for recording and analysing match activities, some form of shorthand was needed to record events accurately. The need arose because activities occurred too rapidly for them to be noted manually with any degree of accuracy. One approach was to record matches on film or video tape and review the game subsequently. This was the strategy for the family of methods that became known as motion analysis. An alternative was to adopt a system of coding those activities that were characterised as relevant to an assessment of performance in the game, which would allow the events to be notated and later collated. This line of approach has been termed *notation analysis*.

Most systems of notational analysis focus on the players engaged in activity with the ball and on strategic/tactical aspects of performance. The most commonly employed systems are pen and paper based and involve a form of shorthand notation using tally marks or action codes (Table 1.1). Positional data may be recorded by breaking down a schematic pitch representation into numbered zones. The position (where?), the players involved (who?), the action concerned (what?), the time (when?) and the outcome of the activity (e.g. successful or unsuccessful, or on target or off target) are recorded. The analysis is then moved on to the next immediate point of action or contact with the ball – for example, who made the tackle, in which part of the pitch, at what moment in the game and was

Table 1.1 *A simple tally sheet to record frequency counts on shots and dribbles*

Player	Shots		Dribbles	
	On target	Off target	Successful	Unsuccessful
Roberts	✔✔✔	✔✔	✔	✔✔✔✔
Smith	✔✔	✔✔✔✔		✔✔

possession gained? This information provides basic match counts which can then be assessed for success rates of actions such as headers, tackles, passes and shots for individual players. A less frequently used alternative strategy is to concentrate on movement of the ball. Data can be registered for the frequency of contact, number of touches or passes in a move before possession is lost, the speed of ball movement by each team, and so on. The resultant information, along with data regarding position on the pitch, can yield valuable insights into the intensity as well as the pattern of play. Various systems have tended to record the number of actions in attacking sequences in order to look at the playing styles and determine whether direct or possession play is more useful in creating scoring opportunities.

Modern systems enable data to be entered using a computer. The mouse and a specially adapted keyboard are the most common means of entering data, although voice recognition may also be used. The developments in digital video recording have also enhanced the facilities for notation analysis. The material can be coded online and integrated quickly into an overall summary. Events during play can be highlighted and, if appropriate, extracts can be shown to the team or individual at half-time or after the game. The use of a time code allows immediate access to any specific time or action within the recording, allowing optimum use of player/coach time. Such an application underlines the potential for the information extracted to be used in altering behaviour during the second half of the same game.

Motion analysis

Motion analysis is focused on raw features of an individual's activity and movement during a match without attempting any qualitative evaluation. Its origins are in ergonomics rather than dance and it reflects attempts to relate work-rate of individual players to its physiological consequences. The original form of time-and-motion study was a device to quantify industrial output and form an objective basis to increase productivity. The system gave rise to the use of 'piece rates', whereby workers were paid according to their output. The approach was known as 'work study' and lost appeal as ergonomics investigations placed the human operator in a central position and recognised the need to fit the task to human capabilities. In much the same way, the analysis of a player's performance can indicate either the demands imposed by the game or the upper limit of the player's self-imposed demands.

Various methods of motion analysis have been applied to the study of soccer. The classical method utilised a coded map of the playing pitch and cues along each sideline to help estimate distances covered by the one player under observation (see Figure 1.1). Activities

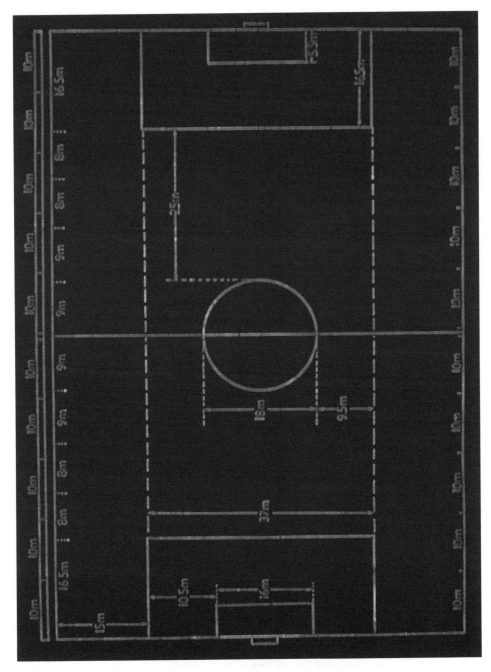

Figure 1.1 *Outline map of the pitch utilising background cues for estimating distances*

were broken down into discrete events and rated according to intensity, such as sprinting, cruising, jobbing, walking, and so on. A running commentary of events was recorded on tape and later transcribed for collation. The method was validated by simultaneously video-recording the locomotion of the same player and counting stride frequencies at each intensity, distance per stride at each category of activity having been previously calibrated.

The method has proved to be sensitive in identifying fatigue, differentiating between positional differences in work-rate (Figure 1.2) and fitness levels. The method is still applicable today but requires care and attention in its implementation. A strategic vantage point, elevated well above ground level and ideally overseeing the half-way line, should be chosen. The objectivity of the operator and the reliability of the method need to be established for the analysts in question. The zoom lens may be used if counting stride frequency is adopted; otherwise, changing the focal length of the camera lens is likely to introduce error into the calculations.

An alternative approach was adopted by Japanese researchers who used synchronised cameras, one operating in each half. The cameras were linked by potentiometers so that location and movement of a player could be traced on a scaled map of the pitch. Computerised analysis allows distances of each movement, accelerations and decelerations to be calculated, the filmed activity being linked to a time base.

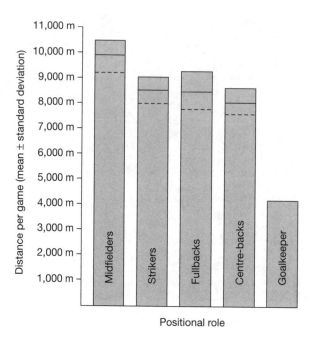

Figure 1.2 *Distance covered in a game according to playing position (based on T. Reilly and V. Thomas, 'A motion-analysis of work-rate in different positional roles in professional football match-play'.* Journal of Human Movement Studies, 2: 87–97 (1976))

Contemporary computer-aided analyses allow the movements of an individual player to be tracked by determining the x, y coordinates of the player's location at the start and end of discrete activities. This approach requires a scaled map of the pitch onto which the filmed activity can be superimposed. The error associated with this method is theoretically small, but needs practice to reduce operator error. The more sophisticated contemporary systems utilise multiple cameras fixed in position on the stands. Typically, three cameras are employed along the roof of each main stand. Activities of all the players are captured on camera and the principles of both notation analysis and match analysis can be used in extracting data from the filmed record. The original system was developed by Sport-Universal Process and implemented in support work for the national team in France. Later versions and upgrades have been used in the major European national championships, including the clubs of La Liga (Spain) and the Premier League (England). The system tends to be sold as a service to the clubs installing the cameras on their home grounds. Whilst vast quantities of data can be generated during a game (see Figure 1.3), their reliability and validity have not yet been satisfactorily established.

Global positioning systems have some promise for the systematic recording of players' locomotion during training and matches. Such an approach has been used to study the US women's team. The system to be applied requires careful calibration for the stadium concerned, and the magnitude of error depends on the number of satellite connections. Although currently applied to monitor the movements of Australian Rules footballers in practice contexts, it has not been adopted to any significant extent by soccer coaches.

A limitation of the systems outlined above is that the analysis and interpretation of observations are done after the event. The extraction of data can be painstaking and susceptible to unknown systematic and human error. It is likely that current developments in engineering technology will make available facilities for real-time analysis of data. For example, ultra-wideband radio-frequency techniques could provide a method of monitoring the locomotion of participants in competition and in training. The approach would require the tagging of individual players electronically and tracking their movements by means of radio transmitters and receivers positioned around the pitch. Speeds and distances could be measured from the coordinates obtained, for players and also the ball. Whilst the technologies are currently available for such tracking systems to be designed for field games, the existing rules of competitive play may restrict their developments.

The work-rate profile indicates the gross physical contribution of a player to the total team effort. The work-rate of individual players can be indicated by the distance covered in a game, although this is only a crude measure of work-rate in soccer. The many changes in activity during match play raise the energy demands imposed on players above those associated with orthodox locomotion. During a soccer match an individual player will perform a wide variety of activities ranging from walking slowly to sprinting maximally. These changes involve not only alterations in the pace and direction of movement but also the execution of skills such as dribbling, tackling, heading and shooting. The exercise pattern can therefore be described as intermittent with maximal efforts superimposed on a background of low-intensity exercise. By far the greater part of the distance completed during games is performed at low intensities (walking and jogging). High-intensity (cruising and sprinting) activity is relatively infrequent and short in duration. These highly

Distance Covered (KM)

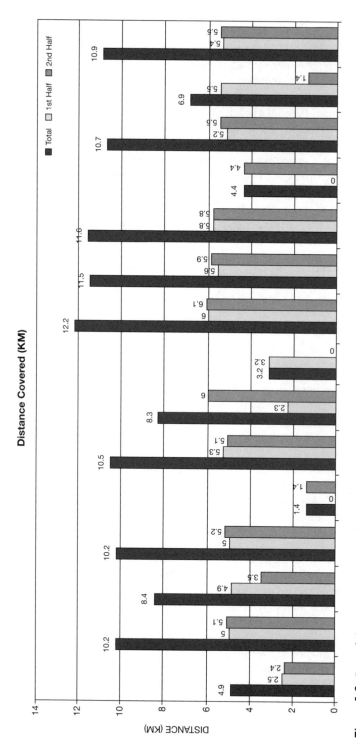

Figure 1.3 *Part of the computer output showing overall distances covered in the first and second halves by players from two teams in the English Premier League in one game*

intense activities can, however, be crucial to match outcomes as they relate to actions such as quick moves into space to receive a pass or act as a decoy, movements to win the ball and movements with agility to go past defending players.

Imposed on an individual's activity profile are the game's skill elements. These elements range from throw-ins and corner kicks to tackles, passes, shots and headers, reflecting players' direct involvement in the match. Less than 2 per cent of the total distance covered by elite players is covered whilst they are in possession of the ball. The vast majority of the actions performed during a game are 'off the ball', either running to create space or support team-mates in possession of the ball, or tracking opposing players and running to contest possession. These figures slightly underestimate the players' direct involvement in the game as the distance covered with the ball does not include engagements in single contacts or physical duels with an opponent. Frequency counts have been employed in an attempt to analyse the occurrence of specific match actions (e.g. controlling the ball, heading, passing): for example, the mean numbers of headers and tackles were 8.9 and 10.9 for Danish players, 9.9 and 13.1 for Australian players and 9.0 and 14.0 for Swedish players. Only half of the total of the 51.4 ± 11.4 ball contacts are with the foot (26.1 ± 12), with turns (49.9 ± 13) occurring more frequently than jumps (9.4 ± 6.5).

The overall work-rate and hence the physiological demands vary with the level of competition, playing style, positional role and environmental factors. International-level match play imposes different technical and tactical restraints on players as compared with domestic club competitions. Such changes may have direct consequences for an individual's work-rate profile. The demands associated with international soccer match play have also been related to individual anthropometric profiles of players.

In summary, work-rate methodologies are based on the principle that the energy cost of moving a given distance is directly related to mechanical work output and is largely dependent on the speed of motion. The work-rate of individual players can be indicated by the distance covered in a game. The total distance covered reflects the overall intensity of exercise, and also the individual contributions to the total team effort. The intensity of effort can be coded as sprinting and cruising (running sub-maximally with obvious purpose and effort), jogging, walking and assuming a stationary posture. Jumps and tackles, dribbling with the ball, moving sidewards and backwards, making angled runs can also be recorded. The ratio of high-intensity to low-intensity exercise can also be calculated since it can give an indication of the recovery pauses available to players during the game.

WHY MATCH ANALYSIS IS UNDERTAKEN

The coaching context

So far, certain features of soccer play have been described and a background to the use of match analysis has been provided. The major methods of match analysis were detailed, and separated into systems for motion analysis and notation analysis. There still remains a rationale for the use of match analysis and an argument for its adoption by coaches to support their work. Probably the main aim of match analysis when observing one's own team's performance is to identify strengths which can then be further built upon and weaknesses which suggest areas for improvement. Likewise, a coach analysing opposition performance will use data to try to counter opposing strengths and exploit weaknesses. Match analysis can also be used to evaluate whether a training programme has been effective in improving match performance and record performance over a period of time. Information stored in databases can help create a benchmark against which future performance can be compared. The match analysis process is described in more detail in the remainder of the chapter and some of the factors influencing observation and data interpretation are mentioned. In this book, guidelines are provided to enable coaches to develop their own match analysis system and discover how to use available resources effectively.

The coaching process

The coaching process generally comprises a number of steps or cycles, as highlighted in Figure 1.4. Coaches initially evaluate performance prior to planning and implementing practice sessions in an attempt to improve performance in the next match. Before implementing practice, feedback on performance is vital if players are to improve. Feedback can be acquired intrinsically, through the player's own sensations, or extrinsically, through a coach. The match analysis process tends to concentrate on the latter by analysing, evaluating and providing feedback on completed actions and movements. It is the responsibility of the coach to ensure that the best possible feedback is provided. This feedback can be given quantitatively through statistical analysis or qualitatively through the use of video recordings or match reconstructions. Feedback should above all be constructive, positive, provided at the right time and in the right amounts, should relate to the player's skill level and should allow the development of a model for comparison.

The coach's evaluation of performance is typically based on his/her observation, analysis and interpretation of the preceding match, or at best over a series of matches. However,

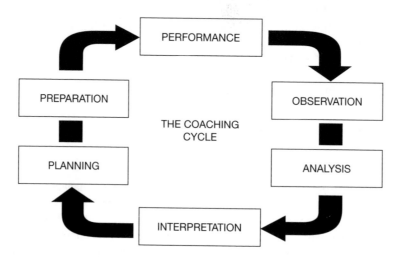

Figure 1.4 The coaching cycle, highlighting the importance of observation and analysis

research indicates that coaches are able to recall fewer than half of the key incidents that arise during a game. The coach's recollection of the match is affected by several factors, such as:

- viewing environment (coaches, like spectators, tend to follow the ball and miss off-the-ball information, and their viewing position is poor);
- limitations of human memory (human memory is limited and it is impossible to remember every single action during a match; also, 'highlighting' is a problem – coaches only remember the key events of a match, which will give them a distorted impression of performance);
- set views and prejudices (some coaches only see what they want or expect to see);
- effects of emotions such as stress and anger (these affect concentration and may distort a coach's impression of the match).

Because of these limitations, it is important that coaches should try to avoid making decisions based purely on their subjective evaluation of performance. An error in observation and evaluation of match performance would clearly have 'knock-on' effects on the effectiveness of the remainder of the coaching process. Consequently, coaches should try to gather as much information as possible in order to base their decisions on objective data (e.g. quantitative match analysis data) or an independent record (e.g. video footage) of performance rather than merely on personal recollection.

What should be analysed?

Most aspects of human behaviour can be analysed. Consequently, it is important to determine what to analyse and the reason for doing so. It is worth bearing in mind the well-known saying that 'not everything that counts can be counted, and not everything that can be counted counts'. The art of employing match analysis effectively is that of deciding what information is important and whether it can be used to improve performance. The coach may want to look for performance errors and weaknesses, and therefore be able to suggest areas for improvement. It may be used to scout a future opponent's strengths or help in team selection. Match analysis systems can be designed to collect data on several aspects of performance, embracing technical, behavioural, physical and tactical factors.

Technical aspects

Video footage of players performing technical skills such as passing, shooting and heading can be used to evaluate technique, provide feedback and help design relevant practice sessions. Specialist software packages also exist to help coaches in analysis technique and providing feedback to players (e.g. see www.quintic.com; www.siliconcoach.com; www.dartfish.com; www.pinnaclesys.com).

Behavioural aspects

Although mental factors cannot be assessed directly, they can be inferred from a player's behaviour. Video footage can be employed to assess aspects of behaviour such as 'game-reading' skill, decision-making, emotional state and concentration. Tally sheets can be used to quantify behaviours such as incidence of negative body language or frequency of 'ball-watching'. A similar approach can also be used to assess coaching behaviours during training and whilst observing matches.

Physical aspects

Movement and work-rate studies can reveal much about the physiological demands of match play and training. Such an analysis requires individual players to be tracked (using either video or sophisticated devices involving, for example, satellite tracking or computer chips). This procedure provides detailed information on the time that players spend moving at various speeds during a game or in training. Heart rate and other physiological responses can also be recorded simultaneously with the motion data by using radio telemetry-based systems.

Tactical aspects

Deciding on an effective strategy and tactics to suit the team is perhaps fundamental to successful performance. A *strategy* is the overall plan that is devised to achieve an aim or specific objective and could relate, for example, to the overall style of play adopted by a team (e.g. slow build-up versus a fast, counter-attacking style of play). The strategy is normally achieved via the application of specific *tactics* (e.g. a specific set play or the type of runs made by a particular player). Match analysis can help the coach to determine the most effective strategy and, more commonly, the specific tactics to be employed by providing objective data upon which to base these decisions.

Critical incident analysis

The multitude of events occurring during a game that are captured using video recordings can be examined for a variety of purposes. These include identifying positive features of play, or searching for key moments that indicate why the game was conceded. Individuals may have lost their 'duels' with their opponents or made unforced errors. Change-overs or loss of possession, vulnerability on counter-attacks and so on may be explored using the critical incident techniques.

Computerised notation analysis also has its use in assessment of injury risk in match play. A list of the playing actions isolated for study is shown in Table 1.2 Key incidents were monitored with respect to the degree of injury potential, location on the pitch, home and away, duration of play and other factors by assuming a code for data entry to each prioritised action. Close to 18,000 actions were notated over ten English Premier League matches (see Figure 1.5). Players were most at risk when receiving a tackle or charge, or making a tackle. The risk was highest during the first and the last 15 minutes of a game. This result reflects the intense engagements in tussles for possession in the opening 15 minutes of the match and the possible effect of fatigue in the closing period. The risk was elevated also in specific attacking and defending zones of the pitch where possession of the ball is more vigorously contested. Whilst these trends are of obvious interest to medical and support staff, coaches and trainers should also be aware of them.

Table 1.2 *Codes used by Rahnama et al. (2002a) for analysing playing actions*

Code	Definitions
1	Dribbling the ball
2	Goal catch
3	Goal punch
4	Goal throw
5	Heading the ball
6	Jumping to head
7	Kicking the ball
8	Making a tackle
9	Making a charge
10	Passing the ball
11	Receiving the ball
12	Receiving a tackle
13	Receiving a charge
14	Shot on goal
15	Set kick
16	Throw-in

Reproduced from N. Rahnama, A. Lees and T. Reilly, 'A novel computerised notation and analysis system for assessment of injury and injury risk in football', *Physical Therapy in Sport*, 3: 183–190, copyright 2002, with permission from Elsevier

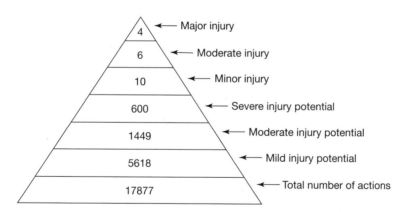

Figure 1.5 *Total actions that were notated, with the number of events in the injury potential and actual injury categories (from N. Rahnama, T. Reilly and A. Lees, 'Injury risk associated with playing actions during competitive soccer'.* British Journal of Sports Medicine, *36, 354–359 (2002), reproduced with permission from the BMJ Publishing Group)*

WHEN TO ANALYSE

Match analysis data can be used to guide team preparation and performance at various stages within the coaching process as highlighted in Figure 1.4. The key stages are before the game, during the match and, finally, afterwards. It is important to mention that when analysing performance, coaches should take into account how their analysis fits into the training and competition cycle. Also, performance analysis can be fitted into an annual plan (both short, medium and long term) such as end of season, pre-season training and friendly matches, after ten competitive matches and halfway through the season. Progress can thus be evaluated at each individual stage.

Pre-match analysis

Information can be collated on forthcoming opponents in the form of match statistics and/or video footage. For example, coaches could collect match statistics to highlight areas where opponents are most effective at making pass assists prior to a goal, the type of delivery that they prefer at corner kicks or how their goalkeeper likes to distribute the ball. An observer or scout can collect such data whilst watching the opponent's matches. Where filmed footage can be accessed, match statistics can be supported with a montage of video clips in order to provide a clearer 'picture' of what to expect from the opposition. Coaches who are better informed about the strategy and tactics employed by forthcoming opponents are more likely to be able to counteract the opponent's strengths and exploit their weakness. This area is surprisingly overlooked, with most coaches preferring to focus on their own team's recent performances rather than those of forthcoming opponents. Such data can also be stored and archived in order to identify how trends and strategies develop over time.

Another rarely used benefit of match analysis is that it can provide objective data for the purposes of player scouting. Coaches and managers often decide to sign a player on the basis of their subjective evaluation of his/her performance during a match, or at best over a series of matches. Occasionally, an opinion may also be sought from another coach or scout as to the player's strengths and weaknesses. There are other instances where managers have signed players without personally observing them in action. Match analysis data on factors such as passing success rate or goal to attempts on goal ratios can help the coach make a more accurate and confident decision as to whether or not the player should be recruited. Coaches can also observe edited highlights or a video montage of the player's performances over a series of matches. With the advent of satellite television, coaches can now observe matches played all round the world, and this information can be used to create dossiers relating to the strengths and weaknesses of specific players.

Some coaches also find it useful to film training sessions using video. The aim is to use the training footage to highlight good aspects of behaviour in training (e.g. attitude, commitment) or to compare aspects of performance that have been worked on in training and how they have been executed during matches (e.g. set plays).

In-game analysis

Simple match statistics can also be collected during a game and used to help make tactical decisions. For example, observers can be asked to record the number of misplaced passes, entries into the final third, missed opportunities to play a cross into the box or times an opponent is left unmarked in the penalty area. Such data can be recorded using simple tally sheets that do not require great effort to complete. Members of the coaching or backroom staff, injured players and even substitutes can be put to good use in this regard. The advantage for the coach is that he/she has objective data upon which to base the half- or full-time 'team talk' or to make various tactical changes and/or substitutions.

Modern digital technology also enables match action to be coded 'live' or from a simultaneous video feed and, if needed, viewed during a match, at half-time or immediately after the game. In England several Premier League teams are currently putting this facility to good use.

Post-game analysis

The vast majority of analytical work is undertaken either immediately after or in the few days following a match. A detailed review of performance can be provided usually within 24 hours of the match and involving both quantitative data and qualitative video footage. This objective analysis can focus on team performance and/or individual players, with this information being employed to set short- and medium-term priorities, possibly in conjunction with the players, for practice and instruction. Such information can be used to reinforce good performance, as well as identifying areas for improvement.

SUMMARY

In a team game, individual members must harmonise into an effective unit in order to achieve the desired result. In such contexts the assessment of how well the team is playing and how much individuals contribute to team effort presents a challenge both to the coach and to his/her back-up sports science support service. Only with objective data can a coach complete an informed judgement about performance within the game.

Both notation analysis and motion analysis techniques, separately or combined, provide a means of evaluating performances of soccer players. The information obtained is a valuable source of feedback to players and coaches. It yields important data with respect to the demands that involvement in the game imposes on players, whose performance capabilities are influenced by fitness factors and the demands they are voluntarily prepared to impose upon themselves. The performance profile can be scrutinised for changes as the game or season progresses in order to identify factors such as the onset of fatigue or the impact of tactical alterations. Surveillance information may also be provided by examining the trends in the style of play used by forthcoming opponents.

CHAPTER TWO

▼ DEVELOPING A MANUAL NOTATION SYSTEM

INTRODUCTION

As illustrated in this book, match analysis systems are becoming increasingly more sophisticated and complex, mirroring quite closely the rapid developments in technology generally. Whilst computerised systems can potentially reduce the workload involved in analysing matches and enable information to be stored in databases, often with accompanying video footage, such systems are nonetheless very expensive and remain an option for only the wealthiest clubs. Fortunately, however, manual, hand-based notation systems can be developed very easily, providing answers to questions posed by the majority of coaches. Such notation systems are cheap (they use pen and paper) and adaptable (they can be personalised for a coach's own requirements), and simple data sets are readily available for dissemination. In this chapter we provide an introduction to manual notation systems, illustrating how they can be developed and evaluated. There are typically four stages involved when using a hand-based notation system: deciding what information is needed and why, designing the hand-based notation system, checking on the accuracy of the data, and collating and presenting the findings.

DECIDING WHAT INFORMATION IS NEEDED AND WHY

It is essential that coaches spend sufficient time considering what information is needed and why. A well-designed system provides the coach with accurate and reliable information that is easily gathered and has an impact on subsequent practice and performance. The information should be of value such that there is a clear link between the analysis undertaken and the coaching process. This is the most important guiding principle to help coaches avoid wasting valuable time and resources. Although different data can be collected from one game to the next, it is vital for this information be integrated within the coaching process.

The match analysis process should provide information about how a team or individual has performed such that it aids the coaching process and helps facilitate performance. If coaches are unable to use this information, whether on the training field or in the dressing room, it is of no practical value. Systems should be developed relative to the specific coaching process that they are intended to support. For example, if a coach is working on defensive aspects of performance in training, then information relating to the team's success in the opponent's half of the field may have limited value. The information must match the purpose for which it is intended. If the team has created few goal-scoring opportunities from crosses in recent matches, match analysis data may be useful to provide objective information as to the underlying causes of this perceived problem. Could this problem be due to difficulties in getting the ball out to the flanks or in poor delivery into the penalty area or a reluctance to cross the ball when an opportunity arises? Objective data can help resolve this issue, providing coaches with information to enable him/her to design suitable practice sessions in an attempt to rectify the problem(s). Similarly, in order to identify the reasons for the team's defensive vulnerability at set plays, a hand-based notation system may provide some information to help the coach provide corrective feedback and to develop suitable sessions.

Finally, in addition to having a clear understanding of the information to be notated, it is important to consider the information that the coach has decided not to notate or is for one reason or another unable to notate. The omission of certain information may create a somewhat incomplete picture. The process of developing an effective manual notation system is about recognising what information will be ignored or missed by the observer as much as it is about identifying what will be recorded. For example, a lack of goal-scoring opportunities from crosses may reflect the forward players' inability to create space inside the penalty area as opposed to the team's difficulty in using the entire width of the field or the poor delivery of the ball into the danger area. Clearly, if the coach is without access to all pieces of the jigsaw, the picture may be incomplete, increasing the likelihood that the match analysis system will be ineffective. The key issue is that coaches should consider what is and what is not being measured when designing the notation system and evaluating the usefulness of the data.

HOW TO DESIGN A HAND-BASED NOTATION SYSTEM

The most commonly employed systems are pen and paper based. These involve a form of shorthand notation of specific match features. Such notation may be undertaken as the match progresses, or immediately after the match if access to a video recording is possible. The quantity of information required by the coach determines whether this is best coded during or after the match. One or more observers may be used to code the same or different features of the match, and the coding may be undertaken by one of the substitutes, the coaching or backroom staff, or a relative or friend, provided that they have some degree of familiarity with the system and understand what specifically needs to be notated. The coach and analyst(s) need to have a clear and shared picture of the information that is required and how this is to be notated. The analyst should initially experiment with a few ideas on paper, undertake several 'live' trials and gradually refine the system until satisfied. The complexity of the system should be increased in logical and easy stages. Refining of the system or adding new bits of information should not take place until the analyst is fully satisfied with how well the system is operating and only after feedback has been obtained from the end-user.

It is also important to understand that there is a wide range of performance actions and outcomes in soccer, and they tend to follow a logical path. This means that when a coach or analyst is collecting statistical data, the process must be structured to allow for or limit the many different possibilities. For example, a pass can be classed as being successful if possession is retained and unsuccessful if possession is lost. The pass can also be further broken down into long/medium/short, in the air/on the ground and favoured/non-favoured foot. A sequence of play can include many different actions such as passes, controls, dribbles, shots, saves and clearances. These action sequences can be recorded using a logical structure within the match analysis system. As they can and often do vary, it is useful to think about creating a structural model in order to define all the possible action types and outcomes in order not to miss any data. For example, Figure 2.1 demonstrates a player who is just about to come into possession and shoot at goal. This example shows how a simple action can become complicated as a result of all the possibilities and

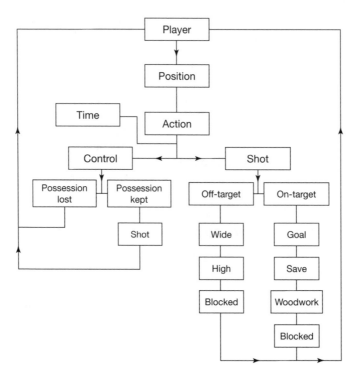

Figure 2.1 *The analysis process for a shot at goal*

outcomes. The figure also strengthens the argument that the initial choice of data to be recorded is essential. The analyst first records the player's name, position and time (see further on in the chapter for more information on these core elements). The action type is then noted; in this example, either the ball is controlled or a first-time shot is made. If a ball control is attempted, then the action's outcome is recorded. For example, if possession is lost (e.g. through a tackle), then the process starts again, or if the ball control is successful then the player will shoot (and again at least the position and time should be recorded, as a new action is now taking place) and the outcome of the shot will then be analysed. If the player decides to shoot first-time after receiving possession, the outcome of the shot must then be noted, as either on target (e.g. goal, save) or off target (e.g. wide, high). Whatever the outcome, the process will start again (e.g. if the ball is saved and goes out for a corner, the goalkeeper, position and save plus action time will be notated).

The basic components in almost every match analysis system are player, action and position. More sophisticated systems may also measure time and sequences of events.

Player

It is often necessary to know which player performed specific actions. When a hand-based notation system or tally sheet is being designed, every player may need to be included on certain occasions. For example, when a coach is attempting to determine why the team loses possession of the ball too frequently, it may be useful to record the pass success rate of all players. At other times, a coach may only be interested in a specific player or group of players and consequently the analysis process is simplified markedly. For example, if a coach is mainly interested in the number of crosses that the team played into the penalty area, then only data for the wide-midfield players and fullbacks may be required. Similarly, a coach interested in the team's perceived weakness in the air at the back may only require information on the headers won or lost by the two centre-backs. An example of a simple notation sheet involving two central midfield players is highlighted in Table 2.1. The data may indicate a weakness in the ability of this pairing to win the ball in the air, although this issue needs to be considered within the context of the match or, more likely, a series of matches. Such tally sheets can be created using pen and paper or via a basic word-processing or graphics software package.

Table 2.1 *A simple notation sheet with only a couple of players included*

Player name/number	Tackles		Headers	
	Won	Lost	Won	Lost
Smith	✔✔✔	✔✔	✔	✔✔✔✔
Jones	✔✔	✔✔✔✔		✔✔

Note: Such a tally sheet could be used to notate any technical action. More complex sheets could include additional columns to record the area (i.e. zone) of the pitch where each challenge occurred and/or the match could be divided into 15-minute time periods.

Action

A range of actions can be recorded such as passing, attempts on goal, crossing, tackles and heading, depending on the interests of the coach. It may also be necessary to record the consequence of each action (e.g. successful or unsuccessful pass or cross, shot at goal – on or off target). This latter consideration can actually be a fairly difficult process. For example, how does one define a 'successful' pass or cross? Is a successful pass one that reaches a team-mate or does the pass also have to be weighted in such a way that the player can control the ball without altering his/her running stride? What is the difference between a successful, yet safe pass to a team-mate in the midfield area and a risky, yet unsuccessful pass that almost creates a goal-scoring opportunity in the final third? Such issues need to be clarified in advance so that both the analyst and the person interpreting the data are consistent in their definition of key terms.

Tally chart tables can also be employed by coaches to collect data for player actions based on a 'success/failure' index. A simple tally sheet (Table 2.2) is used to record frequency counts of unsuccessful and successful actions. At the end of the match, the analyst counts −1 point for each unsuccessful action and +1 point for each successful action. Care should be again taken, as some of these actions may involve personal interpretation, especially if specific match criteria are not clearly defined. In this example, a defender scored an index of 5 and this can be compared over several matches to look at performance consistency and identify various strengths/weaknesses.

Table 2.2 *A simple tally sheet to record frequency counts to create a success/failure index*

	Successful actions	Unsuccessful actions
Tackle	✔✔✔✔✔	✔
Header	✔	✔✔✔✔
Interception	✔	
Clearance	✔✔✔✔	
Free kick (won/conceded)	✔	✔✔
Total	+12	−7

Facets of performance can also be assessed by observing and recording other factors. For example, the number of shots on target or number of crosses played into the penalty area by the opposition may provide the coach with information on his/her team's defensive strengths or weaknesses. Similarly, an analysis of the number of counter-attacks launched against his/her team may tell the coach something about the team's susceptibility to this method of attack. Studying the opposition can often provide a coach with as much, if not more, information than analysing his or her own team.

Position

Invariably, coaches will need to know where on the pitch the action occurred. For example, the fact that the opposing team played ten crosses into the penalty area may be less important than finding out what area of the field these crosses were played from. Positional data may be recorded by breaking down the pitch into numbered zones or cells, as highlighted in Figure 2.2. Alternatively, coaches can use a schematic of the pitch and mark on this diagram where each event (e.g. cross) took place. In a simplistic form the coach may only be interested in very coarse data such as when looking at the balance of crosses played from the right- and left-hand sides of the pitch respectively. In this latter instance, two columns in a table or a simple schematic of the pitch divided into separate zones on the right and left side as highlighted by the shaded area in Figure 2.2 would suffice. Clearly, such a notation sheet can be used to record both teams' crossing opportunities.

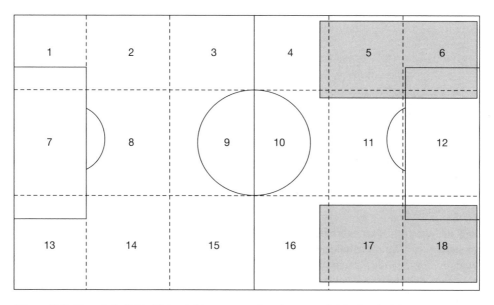

Figure 2.2 *The pitch divided into eighteen zones. Coaches may divide the pitch into as many zones of varying size and shape as needed to get the information they require. Coaches who are interested in the relative proportion of crosses coming from right and left sides of the field may only need two zones as highlighted by the shaded areas*

Figure 2.3 provides another example of how coaches may design schematic notation sheets. This schematic may be used to examine a team's creativity outside the penalty area. The letters A to F could be included in an attached table, enabling the coach to add the names of players, nature of the delivery and outcome of the pass. If interested in where the ball was delivered into the penalty box, the coach could further subdivide the penalty area into zones. Alternatively, the starting and end point of each pass may simply be drawn on the schematic.

The more complex the data, the longer they take to collect and process, so observers should record only what is needed. Coaches should resist the temptation to code everything. Simple notation systems that focus on a small number of actions that are relevant to the coach are of greater value than those that produce reams of data – more is not always

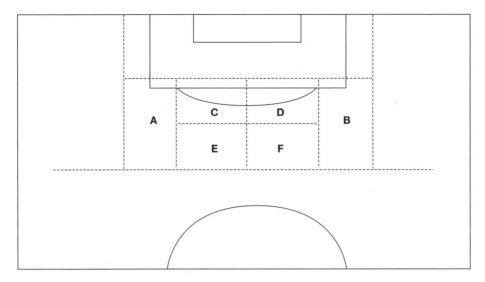

Figure 2.3 *Schematic tally sheet that could be used to determine the frequency count of passes from central areas into the penalty area*

better, so far as match analysis is concerned. Moreover, a well-designed system will only provide the information that it was intended to produce; it does not guarantee success, and the art of coaching is that of interpreting and applying the information in the most appropriate manner!

Consider the following examples. Table 2.3a shows a basic tally chart that records the frequency with which defenders are making tackles, headers or clearances. Table 2.3b provides similar information but in a sequential order so that later analysis can consider sequences of actions as well as their frequency. The method of recording data used in Table 2.3b provides the coach with more information but means that subsequent analysis takes longer. In determining the most appropriate method for recording data the coach must consider:

- the attention required to make an entry onto the sheet;
- the speed with which data can be entered;
- the ease of collating the information at the end of the analysis;
- whether both teams can be analysed by the same person.

Table 2.3a *A simple tally sheet to record frequency counts of key match actions per player*

Player	Tackles	Headers	Clearances
5	A, B, A, A, A, C, D, B, A	D, C, D, C, A, C, D, B, A, A	C, C, C, D, C, D, B, A
7		D, D, C, A, B, F, F	
4	B, A, B, C, C, C, D, B, A		B, B, B, A, A, B, B, A

Note: The letters A to F represent zones as per Figure 2.3

Table 2.3b *A more complicated notation sheet for recording the frequency of crosses (X) and passes (P) in sequential order*

Player and sequence of events	Zone		Action	Possession	
	Start	End		Lost	Maintained
11	5	12	X	✔	
5	8	10	P		✔
6	8	4	P		✔
7	18	12			✔

Note: The sheet allows the recording of added information related to the start and end position of each action and whether possession was lost or maintained.

Time and sequence

Coaches may sometimes be interested in the time course of events. For example, a team may be conceding goals late in the game, and consequently a coach may wish to determine whether the team loses possession of the ball in the final third more frequently in the final 15 minutes of the match or whether there is a drop in the number of challenges being won in that area of the pitch. The coach may divide the game into varying time segments depending on the question of interest. Data can be collated for each half, every 15 minutes or for the last 10 minutes of the match only. Table 2.4 provides an example of a notation sheet where key match actions are grouped in 15-minute periods. A more sophisticated notation sheet is presented in Figure 2.4. This sheet was developed by Howard Wilkinson, when he was Technical Director of the Football Association, for use with the national youth squads. Many coaches are interested in entries into the final third to examine which team has been on top in the game and at what periods. Figure 2.4 can be employed to record frequency counts for entries into the final third, corners (C), free kicks (F), throw-ins (T), crosses (X's) and strikes on goal for both teams in every minute of the match. This table can also be modified to examine the sequence of attacks in a match. Rather than recording entries into the final third per minute, this can be done in sequence/order.

The types of analysis proposed in Tables 2.1 to 2.4 and in Figure 2.4 could potentially, after some training, be notated in real time as the match evolves, thereby providing access

Table 2.4 *Frequency count to indicate the number of times the team gives the ball away through a bad pass (lost possession) and loses a tackle or header (challenges)*

Time period (mins)	Lost possession	Lost challenges
0–15	✔✔	✔✔✔✔
15–30	✔✔✔	✔✔✔✔✔✔
30–45	✔	✔✔✔✔
45–60	✔	✔✔✔✔
60–75	✔✔✔	✔✔✔✔✔✔
75–90	✔✔✔✔✔✔	✔✔✔✔✔✔✔✔

SEQUENTIAL MATCH ANALYSIS FORM

Date:

Team: Team:

Entries	C	F	T	X's	Strikes	MIN	Strikes	X's	T	F	C	Entries
						1						
						2						
						3						
						4						
						5						
						6						
						7						
						8						
						9						
						10						
						11						
						12						
						13						
						14						
						15						
						16						
						17						
						18						
						19						
						20						
						21						
						22						

Figure 2.4 *Tally sheet used to record entries into the final third of the pitch in a sequential order for both teams*

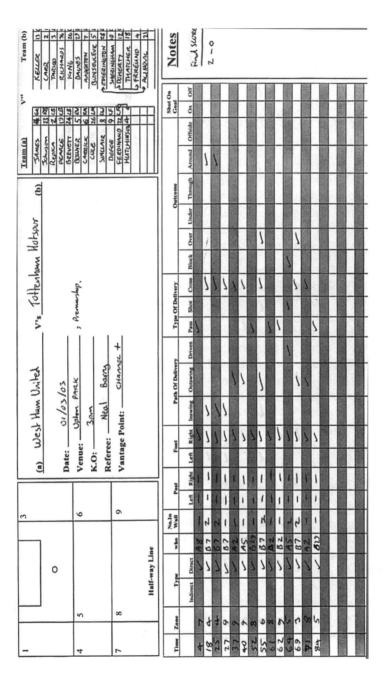

Figure 2.5 Completed analysis sheet for free kicks. Coaches are asked to indicate where the free kick was delivered, whether the free kick was direct or indirect, the nature of the delivery and the outcome

to collated information at various times during (e.g. half-time) and immediately after a match. A more sophisticated and detailed analysis sheet is presented in Figure 2.5. Whilst this sheet provides a wealth of data in relation to the effectiveness of various set plays for and against, it would probably be very difficult to record this information during a match. Such information may best be recorded and collated post-match using video footage. There is a clear trade-off between the level of detail required and the speed with which such information can be provided.

DETERMINING THE ACCURACY AND RELIABILITY OF THE DATA

Some of the classifications employed may be fairly subjective (e.g. successful or unsuccessful cross, long or short pass, dribble or run with the ball) and coaches need to provide clear definitions to indicate, particularly for other observers, what they mean by each category of action. Even so, there is still considerable scope for error in observation and coding. In particular, there is evidence to indicate that an observer's expectation of what he/she expects to see can alter the nature of the coding process. Also, an observer's definition of a specific event may drift or alter over time.

To ensure that the data are objective and reliable, it is helpful to ask another coach to analyse the same match simultaneously. Alternatively, if video footage is available, coaches can review various aspects of the match themselves to ensure accuracy and reliability of the data. It may be useful to compare the real-time notation of the match with that undertaken post-match using the recorded video footage. If time is limited, this can be done for only a portion of the match. Whilst it is not necessary to undertake such procedures every match, it is useful to consider such issues when developing a new notation sheet or when employing a different observer. Once observers have been trained and are familiar with the notation sheet and the agreed-upon definitions of each action, and good agreement has been obtained across observers or for the same observer coding part of the same match, then agreement checks may be carried out less frequently.

COLLATING AND PRESENTING THE DATA

Once the data have been collected, they need to be collated and presented in a simple, easy-to-understand format, particularly if a number of coaches need to access the information. Coaches with a reasonable background in computing can transfer the information contained on the hand-based notation sheet to a data analysis software package such as Excel, thereby reducing the time required to summarise aspects of the data. Coaches without such technical training should try to collate the data as best they can by calculating mean frequency scores and presenting this information in summary tables or in graphical format. The intention is to ensure that other coaches and players can easily access the data. These issues are considered in greater detail in Chapter 5.

SUMMARY

Manual notation systems can quickly provide the coach with valuable information. Such information can be recorded and collated by a coach with limited prior experience and training, and can help inform practice sessions as well as half-time and full-time team talks. The key questions for coaches are what information is required, how this can be recorded in a simple and efficient manner, whether the data are accurate and how this information should be presented to the coach/players. Some of the important issues to consider when addressing these questions are discussed in this chapter. The important take-home messages are that such systems are easy to design, are cost-effective in terms of both time and resources, provide invaluable information and should be used routinely as a fundamental part of the coaching process.

CHAPTER THREE

▼ **VIDEO AND COMPUTERISED MATCH ANALYSIS TECHNOLOGY**

INTRODUCTION

Video and computer technology is advancing at a very fast rate, significantly transforming our lifestyles, and sport is no exception to the rule. The effects of this technology on the analysing, evaluating and improving of playing performance cannot be ignored. The drive for success in soccer, as in many sports, has led coaches to search for the best possible means of improving performance. Many coaches now appreciate the potential of such technology for the analysis of competitive performance and in aiding daily training and preparation. Finding that 'little bit extra' may be the difference between success and failure. This chapter examines the latest video and computerised match analysis systems used in soccer.

VIDEO TECHNOLOGY

Over the past two decades, analogue and, recently, digital video technology have changed the face of the match analysis process. Coaches at all levels can and often do employ video to record and analyse player and team performance. Video analysis can lead to more efficient coaching and quicker learning, with the ultimate aim of yielding positive results on the pitch.

Video has been used for many years now to analyse soccer performance, either in research projects in universities across the world or on a more practical basis by coaches in clubs.

Video has been used for the analysis of technique, tactics and physical fitness, and, to a certain extent, psychological aspects such as anticipation and decision-making. For example, in the 1980s Charles Hughes, the Football Association's former technical Director of Coaching, used video recordings to look at the relationship between tactical patterns of play and shots on goal. Many video-based studies followed in order to verify Hughes' controversial findings, which demonstrated that more shots on goal and goals were produced through direct play. Video was also employed in the 1980s as a means of studying motion analysis in professional soccer. These match analysis studies simply involved the observation of performance using a video cassette recorder and a television monitor to control playback and visualise footage. A further development in this period was the computer-controlled dual video system (CCDVS) created by Winkler in Germany to look at various aspects of individual and team performance. This linking up of video and computer technology was a major stepping stone to today's digital systems. Over the years, many coaches have used video to break down technique (e.g. detecting problems such as players leaning back when shooting) or to look at the behaviour of players (e.g. negative body language). Nowadays, nearly every modern computerised match analysis system uses video as a basis for coding and presenting performance.

WHY USE VIDEO?

Video provides an excellent means of recording, observing, analysing, evaluating and checking performance. The recent development of digital video has further improved these steps involved in the analysis of performance. The benefits of using video may be listed as follows:

1   Video provides a permanent record of performance which can be watched as many times as desired. Many clubs and national federations now have a library of video recordings involving their own team and opposition performance. This archived footage can be used to create presentations using instances of past and current performance.

2   Video provides valuable information that may have been missed or forgotten by coaches and players during the match. Recordings of match performance can help the coach to recall and judge performance better (opinions are not just based on personal memory and opinion), as they provide a permanent and complete record of what happened on the pitch. Coaches analysing video may find that the players have actually performed better or worse than they originally thought. Soccer involves many different performance factors such as tactics and techniques which are constantly interacting, and the difficulty lies in accurately recalling this large amount of information and applying it in the most efficient manner in training.

3   Video can be used to concentrate on any aspect of performance or any particular player. For example, a dedicated camera may be used to film and zoom in on the game of a player to identify technical strengths and weaknesses. Another coach may use video to record and analyse team tactics during set plays. Performance can also be filmed from any angle.

4   Perhaps the most important aspect of video technology is that it provides an opportunity to play back match actions. The coach can repeat the action sequence

Figure 3.1 *Digital video software for viewing match performance (courtesy of Sport-Universal Process)*

as often as is necessary to ensure that the players have absorbed and understood the required information. The action can be played back at different speeds (e.g. slow-motion replay of a counter-attack leading to a goal), paused to highlight a particular issue (e.g. a defender caught out of position or ball-watching) and, if footage is available, viewed from different angles (e.g. such as player positions at a corner filmed from behind the goal). Slow-motion replay is extremely useful when breaking down individual game sequences. For example, a team may have conceded two goals from counter-attacking situations. Using a slow-motion facility, the coach can 'walk' the players through the critical movements and point out positions and actions and the various mistakes made. This information can then be presented against an example of good performance (e.g. an opposition counter-attack was successfully broken down). As mentioned earlier, video is extremely useful for technique analysis, and slow-motion playback will allow the finer points to be examined more closely. For example, top-level goalkeepers may watch footage of the tactics and techniques of opposing penalty-takers, whereas coaches can also provide outfield players with feedback that may further refine technical skills such as passing and shooting.

5 Videos can be used in real time for immediate analysis and evaluation during the half-time break, or post-match for a deeper insight. Film clips can be edited to show only the most relevant information (e.g. a series of set pieces), thereby avoiding a player having to look at non-critical events, therefore optimising player–coach learning time.

6   Video is an appealing and extremely familiar means of presenting and discussing performance during team talks (more so than pure statistical analysis). Players and coaches alike are often more comfortable with video, which will help encourage discussion and the two-way flow of feedback. Although video is often used to highlight problems or mistakes, players can be shown positive aspects of performance in order to gain confidence from seeing themselves doing well on the screen.

7   Individual 'movies' and presentations can be created for players. Huge amounts of information on many aspects of performance will not concern every player and personalising what is shown may improve understanding and learning. Recordings can also be given to players to review edited footage in their own time (such as in the privacy of their own home).

8   For younger players and coaching courses, instances of skilled performance can be used as a basis to demonstrate how 'it should be done' and provide performance-related goals. As post-match video tends to demonstrate what was actually done, rather than what to change, this is extremely important.

9   Digital video enables performances to be recorded onto a computer in real time, then accessed, observed, replayed, edited, re-edited and archived at the simple touch of a button. Through using a time code (electronic indexing method used for editing and timing video programs), this helps to streamline the whole video editing process. Digital video also allows graphical information such as titles and text to be easily added and specific points to be highlighted using, for example, drawing tools or touch-sensitive screens to provide feedback on various aspects of performance. It also offers other advanced editing and visualisation tools such as trimming tools (to cut and provide only the most relevant information), smooth transitions between movies, multiple camera views and window sizes, zoom-in and -out capacity, synchronised split-screen option or the ability to blend two recordings in order to compare two actions at the same time, image snapshot (still picture of a particular action), voice-over, output to tape (for viewing on a VCR) and DVD/CD-ROM for viewing on a laptop, as well as compressed formats for transfer and publication on the Web.

10 Modern-day video equipment is adaptable to any level of user and is generally user-friendly in terms of its set-up and utilisation. It is important to remember that employing video involves a learning curve for both coaches, who must gradually optimise their presentation methods/time, and the players, who must become accustomed to the use of video in match preparation. In addition, the portability of computer video analysis systems has vastly improved, thanks to the development of laptop technology. Laptops can even be brought onto the training pitch to provide immediate information and feedback. Some teams may want to use a mobile-networked solution where players can log onto a portable server containing video footage. This may prove useful when teams are travelling, to provide complementary information on opponents. Detailed information on choosing different types of audio-visual and computer equipment is given in Chapter 4.

EXISTING DIGITAL VIDEO SYSTEMS

Few analogue-based systems are currently in use; computer digital video now dominates the market. Most digital video editing systems also provide statistical match action coding and are sold as 'all-in-one' packages. However, there are different software programs which simply concentrate on providing dedicated match video editing tools. These include SportsEdit (Pinnacle Sports, United States), Videosequencer (Sport-Universal Process, France) and Gamebreaker (Sportecinternational, Australia). All these systems use a digital time code to record the exact moment of various actions in order to facilitate subsequent access, editing and visualisation of match performance. These are extremely powerful feedback tools which are currently used in top-level soccer.

COMPUTERISED MATCH ANALYSIS SYSTEMS

Chapter 2 shows how manual match analysis systems can provide valuable information and data on playing performance. So why use computers if a simple pen and paper system is adequate? Computers aid in the match analysis process at two significant levels: data input and output. The former involves the actual methods employed for inputting or coding match data such as passes or shots, whilst the latter involves the processing and presentation of these data. The advantages of computerised systems compared to manual analysis can be listed as follows:

- Learning time is generally quicker and data input easier, owing to user-friendly computer interfaces and advanced inputting tools such as voice recognition or touch pads.
- Systems can automatically provide useful indications on individual and team strengths and weaknesses and can help propose specifically adapted training methods.
- They can be used to provide even greater detail and more accurate information on all aspects of playing performance and allow advanced statistical analysis of performance.
- They allow statistics to be combined with the match video, allowing immediate access and visualisation of any particular action or moment in the game. This no doubt leads to quicker and better evaluation and understanding of match performance.
- Large databases of past performances can be created for trend analysis over any defined period of time.
- They can be used to provide extremely quick, relevant and objective feedback. Data processing now takes only a matter of seconds.
- Such systems provide any form of easy-to-understand data presentation such as graphs or tables. For example, these can be printed out, or displayed using a video projector during team presentations.
- Computerised systems allow data and video to be copied onto CD-ROM or DVD-ROM or transferred over the Web, hence the information can be read on the road, and indeed anywhere in the world.

However, even the most modern computerised systems can have certain disadvantages and the coach must be aware of these.

- Price can be a stumbling block, even though prices have fallen dramatically over the years. Coaches at the lower end of the game may not be able to purchase the best systems or video equipment.
- Equipment and software may be difficult to set up and use, especially for coaches with limited knowledge of modern audio-visual and computer technologies. Portability can unfortunately still be an issue. Problems may also occur through damage or battery life.
- Data input errors and losses can occur as a result of poor or complex system designs. The system is only as good as the user, and vice versa. Chapter 4 offers detailed information on what to look out for when acquiring a match analysis system, whether this be manual or computerised, as well as providing advice on audio-visual equipment.
- Feedback may be limited to what the system can analyse and how quickly the data can be provided after the match. Also, the coaching staff may not agree with data used to define certain match actions.
- In professional soccer, performance data are generally not collected by clubs for scientific research or experimentation. These data need to be practical and translated correctly onto the pitch. Modern systems can often provide too much information, or non-relevant information. When evaluating data, coaches may also look for problems which do not exist, especially as a result of the vast amount of information now provided by modern systems. A player who shows a slight falling off in one area of match performance should not be judged immediately; further analysis and evaluation may be necessary.
- Players may feel that systems are like 'Big Brother' and that their performances are being dissected too often and too much. The use of match analysis may be an extremely sensitive issue when a coach is working with players.
- When using video, coaches should be careful when comparing and presenting recordings of elite or 'ideal' performance, as a player may have his/her own 'unorthodox' methods which are nevertheless highly successful. Also, these 'ideal' performances may be unattainable for certain players.
- Such systems can lead to an over-reliance on technology. Some coaches and players may feel that their match analysis system is indispensable. However, this is simply one of the components involved in improving performance and is certainly not the only important factor.

In conclusion, computer and video match analysis systems are employed to bridge the gap between performance, observation, analysis and evaluation by helping to create an effective and optimum communication channel between coach and players.

THE FIRST SYSTEMS

Over the past 20 or so years, various computerised match analysis systems have appeared on the market, each offering different and often improved levels of usability and data. The majority of these systems have been developed as various notational research projects in universities, and it is only in recent years that their usage has been truly extended to clubs or national federations. Amongst the first systems were the concept keyboard developed by Church and Hughes (S. Church and M. D. Hughes, 'Patterns of play in association football: a computerised analysis', communication to the First World Congress of Science and Football, Liverpool, 13–17 April 1986) used for analysing playing patterns and a system developed by Partridge and Franks (D. Partridge and I. M. Franks, 'A detailed analysis of crossing performance from the 1986 World Cup', *Soccer Journal*, May–June 1989, pp. 47–50, and *Soccer Journal*, June–July 1989, pp. 45–48) to analyse crossing performance. The former used a specially adapted touch-sensitive keyboard to input match data. The latter was innovative as the results were downloaded into a database which could then be queried to reveal selected results.

Dufour, and Gerisch and Reichelt developed newer and even more powerful software. For example, the former evaluated player and team performance from a physical, technical and tactical point of view. The latter looked at one-on-one confrontations throughout a match whilst linking them to the match video. Finally, Winkler created a system to study performance in both training and competition using two cameras to cover the whole pitch (W. Dufour, 'Observation techniques of human behaviour', G. Gerisch and M. Reichelt, 'Computer- and video-aided analysis of football games', and W. Winkler, 'Match analysis and improvement of performance in soccer with the aid of computer controlled dual video systems (CCDVS)', all in T. Reilly, J. Clarys and A. Stibbe (eds), *Science and Football II*, E. & F. N. Spon, London, 1993). This was the first system that permitted the analysis of all the players at the same time during the whole match. For more information on these and other systems, a list of further reading is provided at the end of this book.

Over the years, these systems have all provided varying degrees of usability and output. However, in what way are the latest systems better? The most obvious answer is based on the advances in technology and the recognition by coaches of the utility of match analysis. The main reasons are listed below:

- Major increases in computer processing power have occurred and vastly improved audio-visual equipment is on offer.
- Much better programming tools are available, and hence better software performance (e.g. in terms of reliability and speed). Overall ergonomic design of both software and hardware has vastly improved.
- Hardware reliability has improved and better overall portability is available.
- Increased communication takes place between modern coaches, software development companies and sports scientists. This has allowed better translation into computer jargon of the practical and specific needs of soccer coaches.
- Through the development and utilisation of older match systems, a thorough diagnosis of their disadvantages or weakness can be made. This of course provides valuable information on where various changes and improvements can and should be made.

Parallel to the improvements in general technology, computerised systems will continue to progress, and Chapter 9 looks in detail at future developments in the state-of-the-art field of soccer match analysis.

MODERN SYSTEMS

As technology is constantly changing, it is important that coaches are familiar with the latest match analysis systems and what type of information they can provide. Table 3.1

Table 3.1 Some of the video and computerised soccer match analysis systems currently on the market

Company	Country	Software	Web site
Digital video/statistical analysis			
Dartfish	Switzerland		
Elite Sports Analysis	UK		
MasterCoach Int. GmbH	Germany		
Pinnacle Systems	USA		
PosiCom AS	Norway		
REM Informatique	France		
Scanball	France		
Softory/Sportweb	Denmark		
SoftSport Inc	USA		
Sportstec	Australia		
Sport-Universal SA	France		
Digital Soccer Project	Italy		
Touch-Line Data Systems Ltd	UK		
Wige Media AG	German		4
Video-based player tracking systems			
Orad	Israel		
ProZone Holdings Ltd	UK	PROZONE	http://www..............
Symah Vision	France	EPSIS Locator	
Sport-Universal SA	France	AMISCO	http://www.sport-universal.com
Electronic player tracking systems			
Abatec Electronic GmbH	Austria	LPM	http://www.abatec-ag.com
Cairos Technologies AG	Germany	Cairos	http://www.cairos.com
Trakus Inc	USA	Digital Sports Information	http://www.trakus.com
Other player tracking systems			
Manapps	France	Stadmaster	http://www.manapps.tm.fr/
Sportstec	Australia	TrakPerformance	http://www.sportstecinternational.com

provides a list of current systems. There are three major types of systems now available on the market, all developed using the very latest cutting-edge technology and having benefited from the practical input and knowledge of top-level coaches.

The systems work on either a real-time or a post-match basis. Real-time analysis allows the match to be analysed 'live' as the events unfold. This requires high skill levels acquired through training and experience. The data are instantaneously available for the coach to use either during the match, at half-time or for immediate feedback after the game. A match analyst working in real time can analyse performance either through a 'live' video recording or simply by watching the match from the stands. Post-match systems involve the match being analysed after it has finished. Such analysis requires the use of a video recording to input data. The advantage of post-match analysis is that the footage can be played back more than once or slowed down. Any doubts or mistakes can be easily rectified by the analyst.

Video and statistical-based analysis systems which do not track player movements can be employed on either a real-time or a post-match basis. Electronic player tracking systems are generally based on real-time analysis whereas computerised tracking systems work post-match. However, if only one or two players are tracked, then real-time analysis is possible. Depending on the system, the delay before the results are available can be relatively short. It can be a few hours, though semi-automatic computerised player tracking systems require a day or two.

Video-based statistical analysis systems

Video-based statistical analysis can be described as being perhaps the *simplest* of all the modern-day systems. As with manual match analysis, the information is based around four factors: *player, position, time* and *action* (see Figure 3.2). The match is recorded using either a digital or an analogue camera and the images transferred on to a computer. In general, the analyst inputs the player's name (by clicking in a list), clicks the player's position on a graphically represented pitch, and inputs the type of action carried out (e.g. pass, shot, tackle). Depending on the system, this analysis can be carried out in real time or post-match. Some systems may not use recordings, as the analyst can code the match in real time at the stadium. However, doing so will only provide statistical information. Most modern systems use digital video recordings which have the advantage of a time code, making the input of time automatic. As the recording is played back, the analyst inputs various actions and the computer automatically records the exact time in the match when they occurred. These actions can then be directly accessed and visualised at the click of a button. This avoids having to search by rewinding and fast-forwarding through the footage (as with a VCR), which is extremely time-consuming.

As mentioned earlier in the chapter, through the input of time, player names and actions in conjunction with the video, a selection of game highlights can be obtained from *video editing*. For example, coaches can *chop up and put together* a digitised video of all the attacking moves leading to a shot and examine every action that a certain player makes with the ball or each particular time the ball was lost. This process means that they can select, extract and visualise the specific information they are looking for. Other

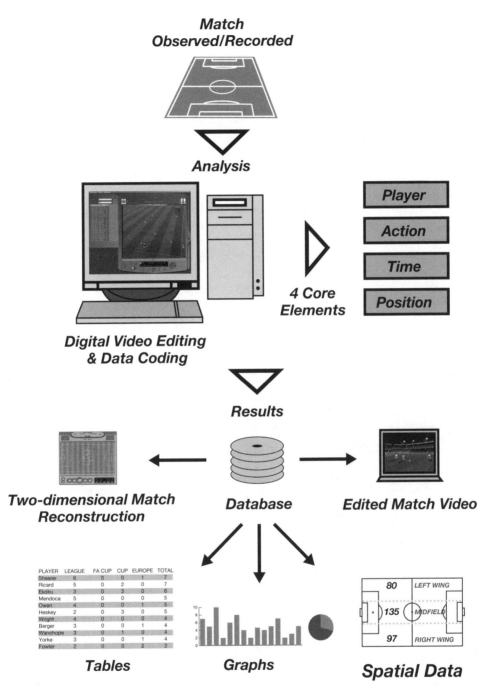

Figure 3.2 *The computerised match analysis process*

data concerning match actions can be presented under different formats such as tables and graphs. More information on the presentation and analysis of results is provided in Chapter 5.

One example of a modern system is the Sportscode digital video analysis system developed by Sportecinternational (Figure 3.3). This system is currently used by many professional soccer teams and match analysis laboratories worldwide. It is described by the company as being fast, results driven, data rich, extremely cost-effective, portable, flexible and user-friendly. One of the major advantages of the Sportscode system is that it can be tailored or personalised for the specific needs of individual coaches. One coach may prefer to concentrate on defensive actions and can therefore customise the interface to include specific coding buttons on the desired areas.

Over recent years, equipment such as touch-sensitive pads and voice recognition have made data input even quicker. Voice recognition is extremely useful as it allows a match analyst to view the game continually and input the data without being distracted by looking for input buttons in the interface. The French sports software company Sport-Universal Process has previously worked on systems using voice recognition to input players' names and actions. First the computer was trained to recognise the analyst's voice. Then the analyst simply spoke into a microphone the name of the player and each game action, and the analyst's words were instantly recognised and recorded by the computer. This reduced

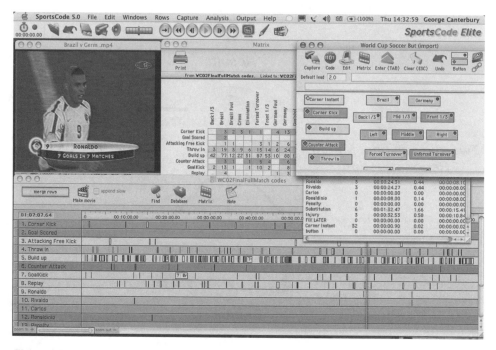

Figure 3.3 *The Sportscode digital video analysis system offers an easy-to-use interface as well as advanced video-editing features and a database of in-depth video and statistical information on team and player performance*

the coding time for a match by at least 10 to 20 per cent compared to classic 'mouse-click' methods.

Small handheld computers can also be used to code match actions using specially adapted analysis software. Their portability and improved user-friendliness mean that they can be used to analyse performance from any position around the pitch. Data can then be easily transferred onto a normal PC for processing and presentation. Statware is one such system developed for coding soccer performance (Digital Scout, United States). These devices are also proving valuable for storing administrative information on players and teams. New-generation mobile phones can also be used to send, receive and display information and statistics on performance. Statistics, alerts and even animations of match actions can be visualised to keep track of performance.

However, video-based statistical systems do have certain limitations. Pitch positions of player actions are determined by simply clicking on a schematic pitch representing the playing area. This procedure will to a certain extent lead to the production of inaccurate positional data. Furthermore, as the video used is often restricted to one camera viewpoint, the performance analysis is limited to only the player in possession and those around the ball. There are further problems if the television footage is used, because of the occurrence of action replays. Whilst the replay is being shown, the viewer cannot analyse the ongoing match play and will probably miss several actions. Finally, these systems do not provide any information on physical performance through player motion analysis. This means that there is also no possibility of recreating and analysing the movements and actions during the match of every single player (two- and three-dimensional reconstructions). This apparent lack of precision and information on movements has led to the development of high-tech player tracking analysis systems which automatically and accurately calculate and recreate player positions and movements.

Video-based player tracking systems

Player tracking systems using the very latest camera, video and computer technology are becoming more commonplace in soccer, especially at the top end of the game. These systems require the installation of several cameras carefully positioned to cover the whole pitch so that every player is always captured on video, whatever his or her position on the pitch and the moment in time. Using complex trigonometry, mathematical algorithms and digital video/image processing techniques, each player's position and movement can be calculated and tracked at every single moment of the game. The AMISCO system, initially developed in 1996, was the pioneer player tracking system and is now used by many top European clubs on the Continent. This system analyses the movements of all players, the referee and the ball ten to twenty-five times a second during the whole 90 minutes. The result is a database for each match containing around 4.5 million positions as well as 2,500 ball touches. Whilst the system design is fairly complex, its functioning can be outlined as follows:

1   A multi-camera system is permanently installed in the stadium using a specially designed program to calculate the number of cameras and their optimal positions required in order to cover the whole pitch. The number and positions of the cameras depend on factors such as the size of the pitch and the structure of the stadium.

Figure 3.4 *The pitch area covered by one particular camera using the AMISCO system (courtesy of Sport-Universal Process)*

2　The stadium and pitch information is calibrated (height, length, width) and transformed into a two-dimensional model to allow the calculation of player positions from the camera viewpoints.

3　At the beginning of the match, the players are initially identified by the analyst. The players are then semi-automatically tracked by the system (some manual input is required from an operator, especially during set pieces) using image processing techniques. A fusion of the 'raw player trajectories' is then carried out to identify and recreate the movements of every player.

4　These positional data also need to be complemented by another analyst, who separately codes the various match actions which cannot be automatically calculated by the computer (e.g. red cards, offsides, tackles). As with normal video-based systems, the input of these actions can be undertaken in real time or post-match.

5　As the data are recorded, they are automatically and progressively loaded into a database for analysis and preparation. The data are then written onto a CD-ROM or DVD-ROM for use by the club. The computer disk contains dedicated software allowing an exact reconstruction of the game in two dimensions as well as a detailed tactical and physical performance analysis of every player. For more information on the results provided by tracking and video systems, see Chapter 5. The whole analysis process is completed within 48 hours.

A positive factor of this type of player tracking system is that players do not have to be equipped with an electronic tag, which up to now has been forbidden by all soccer authorities. However, the difficulty when developing video-based tracking systems lies in finding the optimum positions of the cameras and in accurately tracking many moving objects using complex computer and mathematical techniques. For example, during a corner kick there may twenty players in the penalty area, and the system will require manual input from a match analyst to help the computer identify the players. Furthermore, the system

Figure 3.5 *An example of player tracking by the AMISCO system (courtesy of Sport-Universal Process)*

may be affected by the environment. Heavy snow, smoke and bright light can affect the video footage, although such is the rapid development of these tracking systems that such effects are becoming less of a problem.

The possibility of real-time analysis is generally limited to analysing only a couple of players at the same time or hiring one operator per player, which from a financial point of view is totally unfeasible (22 players plus referee = 23 analysts!). However, it seems that professional clubs are satisfied with receiving the analysis post-match. This is perhaps due to the time required to evaluate, interpret and really make the most of the results, which is not possible during the match itself.

The other major drawback of this type of system is that it can only be used by a team in its own stadium. The video equipment requires time to set up and is not portable and logistically friendly, like a single-camera match analysis system. Teams will have to use classic video match analysis software when they are on the road to provide at least tactical information on performance. However, some clubs equipped with a tracking system may share the results with the away team. In addition, work is needed to develop mini-tracking systems to analyse performance during training, which may prove vital in quantifying the physical efforts of players in order to have a good idea of the workloads experienced. These apparent weaknesses have led to the design and development of new tracking systems using electronic equipment.

Electronic tracking systems

Electronic tracking systems could be described as being the future of the computerised analysis of sport and are taking match analysis one step further in terms of time and accuracy. These systems (based on military radar detection and missile tracking technology) allow real-time data acquisition and analysis and can record performance factors up to several hundred times per second. One such system has been developed in Germany by the technology company Cairos AG. This system was originally developed to aid the referee and assistant referees in making real-time decisions such as whether a ball has gone over the goal line or whether a player is offside. The system tracks the movements and positions of every player and the ball, thereby providing the same information as video-based tracking systems. Its way of working is as follows:

1   A small and very lightweight microchip transmitter is used, which is integrated into the shin pad or shirt of the player, and there is another in the ball. In order to be able to determine the direction of movement, frequency of steps and the length of the step, each player carries at least two transmitters.
2   The positional data concerning the player and the ball are ascertained and evaluated three-dimensionally at the same time and up to 200 times per second within the centimetre range. The identification signal of the transmitter is registered by several antennae in a fraction of a second (the reception time of the signal to the recipient is synchronised and as a result the position is determined). These antennae are positioned around and outside the playing field at various heights (see Figure 3.6).
3   This information is then relayed to the central computer to be processed in real time using specialised software and transformed into a meaningful presentation (e.g. match reconstructions, graphs, tables).

These systems have several major advantages over video-based tracking. First, the analysis (of every player) and data processing are carried out in real time, meaning that performance evaluation is available at any time during the game. Second, the data are perhaps even more accurate (up to several centimetres). Third, the players' movements and positions are analysed several hundred times per second, leading to the production of highly detailed and previously unavailable information on player accelerations and changes in direction.

However, as with video-based tracking systems, the development of electronic tracking has had to overcome various technological difficulties. For example, the microchips have to tolerate extreme stresses such as strong physical contact between players (e.g. a kick on the shin), extreme accelerations such as when a ball strikes a goalpost at 120km h^{-1} or very cold and wet conditions. Previous chips were often too fragile, although the latest versions developed by Cairos have a lifespan of several years. The first chips were also heavier and larger, but their size is being reduced to less than that of a credit card. Also, battery life and recharging are important and progress has had to be made to ensure long life and quick recharging. The current maximum operating duration of a transmitter is now 3.5 hours, which will largely suffice for a match. The telemetric conveying of data has also been known to endure problems through jamming, although specialised built-in protective mechanisms and encoding techniques now prevent this problem. Also, fears of radiation poisoning have had to be allayed!

Figure 3.6 *An example of the stadium tracking equipment set-up (antennae and computer) used by the Cairos match analysis system*

The initial installation at a stadium is also expensive, as it must be accurately measured to the millimetre and the receivers must be coordinated with each other. Furthermore, the stadium must be equipped with special fibre-optic cables. However, once the system is installed, the additional technical expenditure is no longer high and only maintenance work needs to be carried out. Like video-based tracking, the system can only be used by a team at its own ground, therefore another system may be needed to analyse performance in away games. Finally, as Cairos requires players to be equipped with electronic material, negotiations to allow this are currently in process with the relevant soccer governing bodies.

Other player tracking technology

The Stadmaster system is a recent addition to the player tracking field. This system, again based on military hardware and software (optronic technology involving observation, detection, recognition and location of military objectives), is perhaps the easiest to set up and operate of all the tracking systems. A pair of binoculars operated by the match analyst is used to track the exact movements, five times per second, of a single player (more players can be simultaneously followed by other dedicated binoculars). The data are immediately transferred to a laptop computer connected to the binoculars for processing and presentation. The whole process is carried out in real time. The major advantage of Stadmaster, as with video-based tracking, is that players do not have to be equipped with any special equipment. In addition, it is extremely portable and quick to set up (only two operators, a laptop and binoculars are required).

Finally, the rapid developments in global positioning systems have allowed companies to begin their integration into the field of match analysis. A global positioning system receiver uses signals from satellites to pinpoint its exact location on earth at any time and anywhere, and provides information on position, speed and time. These systems are currently used to help configure microprocessor player tracking by mapping out the dimensions of stadiums and pitches. Although at the time this book goes to press, global positioning systems have not yet been adapted for use in the actual tracking of soccer players, they will perhaps be the future of match analysis, as is discussed in more detail in Chapter 9.

DATABASE TECHNOLOGY

The data produced from the match analysis systems referred to in this chapter must somehow be stored in order to be analysed, retrieved, compared and presented in a quick and efficient manner. A database is nothing more than an organised collection of common records that can be searched, accessed, modified and visualised. Databases, which are part of only a few modern systems, also have many other features, as follows:

- They provide an excellent means of looking at past performance by analysing trends over a defined period of time.
- They can store and provide any type of data on demand (e.g. according to time, player, position, action type, speed).
- They can combine data on all aspects of performance, such as physical, technical and tactical information.
- They allow any type of statistical data analysis and presentation through high-quality graphical output.
- Data on several matches can be entered to establish a performance baseline. Improvements following a training programme can then be evaluated by comparing the new data against the original baseline data.
- They can create future performance goals (e.g. greater number of sprints next season and decreased sprint recovery time for a player) and perhaps create predictive models of performance (e.g. repeated and detailed analysis of an opponent's tactical performance will provide a model on how the team plays and the likelihood of its tactical play in future games).
- It is possible to make a database interactive with other databases containing information on areas such as medical and physical assessments. Combining this information can only lead to a better overall understanding of player performance.

A practical example of how a database can help is to look at the physical performance of a player combined with other tactical or technical data. The database can be queried to know how often over a ten-game period the player's work-rate drops at the end of the game (e.g. distance run, number of sprints and recovery times). The database can then provide technical information on the passing success rate as well as positional data at the end of the match. This information can then be graphically displayed to show that the player's performance tended to decrease at the end of the match (low passing success rate and stayed in more defensive areas, hence also contributed little to attacking play). A specific fitness training programme may then be implemented and an analysis of the following ten games can be made in order to evaluate whether the training programme was a success. Care should, however, be taken when comparing data obtained from past performances. Soccer is constantly changing, and data that were recorded a number of years ago may no longer be pertinent. For example, comparing two different cup-winning teams from the 1980s and 1990s is difficult, as many factors have changed (e.g. rules, better equipment, improved fitness and diet). Attention should also be paid when attempting to 'profile' or create a model of performance on how a player or team plays. The number of games chosen, the playing standard and the type of data collected will affect the accuracy of the profile. Information on how to avoid problems when evaluating results is presented in chapter 5.

A database may also be used to store short digital video clips or selected reconstructions of past performance. For example, a coach may want to visualise and present every goal conceded from a set-piece situation over the season. A simple database query will allow these actions to be immediately retrieved and the video clip shown to the players to highlight certain tactical issues. The coach may then ask the database for examples of successful performance (e.g. where the ball was cleared) to demonstrate specific differences.

These performance records can also allow detailed comparisons of the player's abilities for the purpose of team selection and development. For example, trend analysis may lead to the choice of a player's most effective playing position or detect a particular weakness in his/her game and calculate the best possible training programme to improve performance. Expert systems using artificial intelligence may help in these processes by allowing the skilled knowledge, playing and selection criteria of top-level coaches to be transferred into a computer database, which will then provide advice on implementing these criteria in the specific development of the player. For more information on the future of computerised match analysis, see Chapter 9.

SUMMARY

This chapter presents the very latest video and computer technology available in the analysis of performance. This technology has improved the match analysis process at every level, from data acquisition to evaluation and presentation. However, using sophisticated technology is one thing; it is how the coach uses these tools to improve the game that really matters. Coaches should have a good working knowledge of how this technology works and its possible benefits in analysing and improving performance.

It is also important to mention that technology should not become a barrier because it is used in one part of the world and not in another, or by one club and not another. Unfortunately, not every coach has access to this modern technology. Some may not have enough knowledge (or may not even have the desire to learn) regarding how analysis technology can help in improving daily training and match performance. Dedicated education schemes and coaching awards should introduce and help improve the application of this technological facet of modern coaching.

CHAPTER FOUR

▼ **GENERAL ADVICE ON ANALYSING MATCH PERFORMANCE**

INTRODUCTION

Over recent years, coaches have increasingly come to accept the use of match analysis. This acceptance is a result of the gradual acknowledgement that performance analysis has an important role to play in the modern game. Many different systems have been developed for this purpose, both manual and computerised. Coaches may face a dilemma when choosing between match analysis systems, especially when they must justify the outlay. Similarly, both audio-visual and computer equipment play an important part in the analysis process and need to be closely evaluated before purchase. As well as choice of the right equipment, there are various points to respect in relation to preparing for and analysing match performance. This chapter focuses on providing advice on each of these different points.

PREPARATION FOR, AND CARRYING OUT, MATCH ANALYSIS

As with any sporting skill, the process of analysing match performance needs to be practised. Accuracy of match analysis data and reports can only be obtained through well-trained observers using carefully designed and perfected match analysis systems. Therefore, match analysts need to be thoroughly trained to use the system, and practice is a vital part of this education to ensure smooth, efficient and accurate analysis. Similarly, practice is imperative in order to perfect technique when capturing video footage. This section provides advice on preparing and carrying out match analysis work.

Observer training and trials

Any match analysts new to the field should dedicate ample time to becoming familiar with and learning the ins and outs of the system, whether this be a manual or a computerised one. Time investment will yield positive results. The operations manager or usual analyst must spend time presenting the system, showing how it works and providing various tips and information on countering potential problems. It is always worth providing analysts with a user guide if one is available. The more complex the match analysis system, the steeper the learning curve. For example, a manual system using detailed coding for passing and control techniques may require the symbols to be learnt by heart. Similarly, a computerised system using voice recognition to input data may also require thorough learning of similar coding symbols.

Match analysts should initially practise on previously recorded games in order to hone his or her skills. Similarly, getting 'hands-on' practice for manual analysis is prudent and necessary. Post-match analysis differs from real-time analysis. An analyst who has to observe live matches, for example at the stadium, should be placed at least twice in a live practice situation before any official work takes place. It is also worth asking a match

Figure 4.1 *The modern match analyst must be able to use the very latest in video and computer technology. This photo demonstrates the large range of equipment used by the match analyst at the French Football Federation*

HANDBOOK OF SOCCER MATCH ANALYSIS

analyst to analyse the same match twice to compare the reliability of the results. Likewise, it may be worth comparing these results against those obtained for the same match by another trained operator. The reliability of data can be checked by calculating the percentage difference between the sum totals or by correlating lists of results. For more information on how to check the reliability of data, refer to M. D. Hughes and I. M. Franks, *Notational Analysis of Sport: Systems for Better Coaching and Performance in Sport* (E. & F. N. Spon, London, 2004).

Filming match play is an art itself. As with the actual recording of performance data, training and practice are necessary to become familiar with audio-visual equipment. Any coach or analyst wishing to film match play may find attending a specialist video course invaluable.

Analysis preparation

The match analyst needs to be correctly prepared in advance before observing matches at any level of the game. Whether high-tech computer equipment or simple scouting sheets are to be used, there are always various factors to be respected if the analysis is to become efficient and proceed smoothly. The following points are especially relevant for those involved in 'live' analysis or in setting up match analysis equipment.

1   The analyst should try to obtain a fixture list of all the team's matches. This allows a schedule to be organised and planned in advance. Similarly, getting hold of a list of all the squad members' names and pictures can help reduce problems in recognising players. He or she should not hesitate to learn the names of players and their positions by heart, using information previously gleaned from other matches. If two analysts are to be used, always decide on who does what before the match.

2   The analyst should record standard information such as team line-ups in a match summary sheet to help in the post-match analysis and evaluation of results. It is particularly helpful to have this information if it is to be entered into a database of match performance. For example, through noting the playing system of the opposition, a coach may want to look at the results of all the games played against opposition using this type of playing system. Instances of good and/or poor performance can then be provided to optimise the team's chances. Factors which may have affected the playing performance and results obtained (such as environmental conditions) can and should also be recorded. For more detailed information on factors affecting the results from performance analysis, see Chapter 5. Figure 4.2 provides an example of a basic match information sheet. This example shows the major factors which should be noted, such as team line-up and substitutions, date, venue, match type, result, weather and pitch condition, and the referee. A line for general observations is included for any particular point which the analyst feels is important and may need to be taken into account during the post-match evaluation of performance – for example, that the star centre-forward is missing from Team B.

3   Knowing the way and how long it takes to get to a stadium is extremely important in order to arrive with plenty of time to spare before the kick-off. Arriving early

MATCH INFORMATION

Teams: **Team A v Team B**
Match: **Premier League**
Date: **KO 3PM 12 January 2004**
Pitch condition: **Good but 'heavy'**
Referee: **Mr Smith, very strict**

Result: **3–1**   Half-time: **2–1**
Venue: **At home**
Crowd: **Full House, extremely vocal**
Weather conditions: **Very cold & wet**
Observations: **Mea missing for B**

TEAM LINE-UPS

TEAM A Playing System: 4-4-2

Starting Line-up

1	A Smith
2	R Jones
14	B Robert
5	J Dupont (Capt)
3	T James
8	S Johnson
7	T Johnson
11	T Mortimer
16	B Terry
9	O Michael
10	T Gerry

Substitutes

12	T Bianchi (T James – 49 min)
13	F David (O Michael – 85 min)
15	G Owen
17	B Steed
18	A Phillips

TEAM B Playing System: 3-5-2

Starting Line-up

1	B Bead
3	T Green
2	T Town
4	Y Pierre
17	G Jones (Capt)
15	M Day
18	S Chapman
8	M Martin
16	W Gerard
9	K John
11	S Shay

Substitutes

10	T Durand (S Chapman – 65 min)
14	C Spencer (W Gerard – 79 min)
15	G Brown (S Shay – 88 min)
18	E Jackson
19	G Carman

Figure 4.2 *Match information sheet*

allows time to set up equipment and organise oneself and choose a good viewing spot. Also, there may be a need for security passes and to determine whether they allow access to all parts of the ground. If several people are involved in setting up equipment, walkie-talkies or mobile phones may be useful in helping to communicate and stay in contact with others in different parts of the stadium.

4   The choice of an optimal observation position is highly important. The analyst should ensure that he/she has a good, comfortable position with a clear view for the duration of the match. If he/she is observing individuals, a position nearer to the pitch may be required to analyse the players' technique or behavioural factors. If the team's playing system is to be evaluated or data recorded on every player, then a higher view may be much more advantageous (Figure 4.3). What you want to analyse will decide your observation position.

5   If one is analysing performance manually, a ready supply of scouting sheets and writing equipment such as pencils, pens, erasers and sharpeners should be prepared in advance. If sitting, try to take a firm board to lean on when writing. Whatever the required equipment, create a personal checklist so that nothing is missed out.

6   Setting up computer equipment can be a time-consuming exercise. All material should be routinely tested before and after installation. Rebooting the computer

Figure 4.3 *Observation position is paramount. A high viewpoint is advantageous when evaluating team tactics and playing patterns.*

prior to undertaking analysis (especially during the half-time break) can help avoid software problems and crashes by refreshing its memory. Likewise, anti-virus or other software running in the 'background' will use up valuable memory and may cause your computer to freeze. In addition, analysts should be aware that voice recognition, sometimes used to assist in the input and coding of match actions, is affected by background noise.

7   Does the room have enough plug sockets and where are these located? Will the cables be long enough to reach the sockets? Data that have to be sent over the Internet may require a phone line. If several specialised fixed cameras are to be installed such as for modern player tracking systems, these should be set up and adjusted well ahead. Laptop computers and camcorders should always be fully charged up and a spare brought along if possible. In addition to batteries, a charger and AC adapter are useful. An automobile cigarette lighter adapter can be used for recharging equipment. Make sure that enough camera film or memory space is available to record the whole of the game.

8   Take some pre-match sample film footage to ensure that light, position and the camera movements and zooming are fine. The players' warm-up session can be used for this purpose. Finally, make sure that the camera is well fixed or protected so that it cannot be knocked out of position or 'jumpy footage' obtained as a result of wind or supporter movements.

9   The weather can cause havoc with soccer matches, and the same goes for the analysing of match play. If the analysis is to be carried out in an uncovered position on the side of the pitch, then warm, protective and waterproof material and clothes may be required. Try to take into account changes in light. As the match progresses, the analyst may end up with the sun directly in his/her eyes and this will cause observation or filming problems.

10   Finally, the match analyst must be well rested and alert. Observing matches can be extremely tiring as a result of the high levels of concentration required over a relatively long period of time.

Analysing the match

It is important to try to see and note only what is being looked for! Avoid adding any surplus information, as this will lead to difficulties. The analyst must always be objective, neutral and honest. Always stay calm if a mistake is made and try to make a mental or, better still, a written note of the error. Similarly, do not hesitate to record any factor which may affect the results. The analyst can use the half-time break to evaluate personal performance and should, if possible, take time out to rest.

When one is filming the game, it is always advisable to start the recording around 20–30 seconds before the kick-off. Is it possible to see what it is intended for the viewer to see? The analyst must be aware of what is in the shot and what isn't. Use zoom-in and zoom-out features sparingly, as they will produce jumpy footage. Also, footage with rapid pans (camera movement from left to right, right to left) and tilts (up or down movement) is extremely unpleasant to watch and may prevent players from seeing the video recording clearly during the post-match analysis. Manual focus may be advantageous when filming close up, as when observing player technique next to the pitch and if there is a lot of movement of 'dominant' figures. Avoid shaky footage by using a tripod. Many digital camcorders offer an image stabilisation option which minimises the effect of small hand movements. Keep a note on the changes in light. The backlight compensation option allows the camera to compensate for overly bright light or low light.

Post-match

Take time to note down any problems or unexpected issues during the analysis. Methodically and carefully pack away all pieces of equipment. Try to use a checklist to make sure that nothing has been forgotten.

ADVICE ON CHOOSING A PERSONAL COMPUTER SYSTEM

The quality and choice of equipment to run computer software can determine the efficiency of the match analysis process. For example, software for digital video and match analysis requires much processing power and memory capacity, which obviously increases cost. Although a detailed review of all modern hardware and software is beyond the scope of this book, the various factors to be examined when purchasing are briefly listed below.

- *Platform/operating system*: Macintosh (Mac OS) or PC (Windows). Both have advantages and disadvantages as regards price, user-friendliness, compatibility, power and software availability.
- *Microprocessor speed*: Crucial to system performance, a fast microprocessor is always a must for processing information quickly.
- *Memory*: At least 256 MB of RAM is now advised for minimal comfort when running software.
- *Hard drive speed and storage capacity*: The greater the capacity and speed, the more the information that can be stored and quickly accessed.
- *Firewire connection*: Used for connecting digital camcorders to the computer. This is now paramount in transferring digital video between the camcorder and the computer. For analogue camcorders, a special video card for film transfer and digitising is necessary.
- *Computer screen*: A large, 19-inch screen is recommended for analysing matches. However, the larger and better-quality screens (especially flat screens) are more expensive.
- *Printers*: The choice is between laser, inkjet, colour and black-and-white. Price and quality often vary.
- *Digital film editing software*: This varies in user-friendliness and price. Acquiring other software such as Microsoft Excel and PowerPoint may be useful for carrying out data analysis and creating multimedia presentations for match talks.
- *Laptops*: As well as all the above points, price, portability (weight and size) and battery life are the two major issues to take into account when choosing a laptop.
- *CD or DVD writer/scanner*: These vary in price and quality.
- *Internet connection (software/hardware)*: Useful for communicating with other coaches and for searching for information. The faster the connection, the better.

Any good computer store will provide advice on hardware and software issues. The match analyst should take the time to explain what his/her personal requirements are. Furthermore, it is always worth carrying out personal research using specialist magazines or Web sites. Finally, always enquire about equipment guarantees and technical support.

ADVICE ON CHOOSING AUDIO-VISUAL EQUIPMENT

With the advent of digital video there have been enormous benefits for computer-aided and video match analysis. The price of such equipment has gradually decreased, whereas the quality and user-friendliness have increased dramatically. It is not possible to detail all the 'ins and outs' of video and camera equipment. However, it is always worth drawing the analyst's attention to the main points involved in making a choice.

- *Video cassette recorders (VCRs)*: If the analyst prefers to use a conventional VCR to observe performance, then playback quality is the most important issue. Excellent freeze-frame and slow-motion playback facilities are imperative when highlighting specific tactical and technical issues. Also, the VCR should contain a built-in time code generator to aid video editing and locating specific match moments in the tape.
- *Camcorder (digital or analogue)*: First, primary considerations are personal budget and the camcorder's intended usage. Second, the next important decision will be which format is desired, digital or analogue. Digital camcorders, whilst often more costly, provide the most advanced features and quality. They also allow a seamless transfer of video to a personal computer for editing without any loss in quality. Digital video is also endlessly reproducible and will not wear out, unlike tape. If lower-quality video is acceptable and the budget is smaller, an analogue camera will suffice. It is still possible to import video from an analogue camera into the computer. The downside, apart from the time cost, is that when video is transferred to the computer for digitising, there is a loss of quality, owing to the compression formats.
- *Options and special effects*: Resolution, memory, lens, shutter speed, frame rate, zoom, viewfinder, slow-motion capture, still image capture, image stabilisation and sound quality must all be weighed up. It is always worth spending time studying and understanding these options.
- *Portability*: The camcorder should preferably be small, compact and light, as well as being shock-resistant. If possible, look for a model with a waterproof housing. Also, if buying a tripod, this should be strong and portable, and should allow good camera control.
- *Battery life*: Good-quality, long-lasting batteries are needed when filming. Lithium ion batteries generally work well.
- *Video projectors*: Price, display quality and portability are the major concerns.

As when one is buying a computer, any good audio-visual store will provide advice on video and camera equipment. As mentioned earlier, the match analyst should spend the necessary time explaining what exactly will be required. Again, it is always worth carrying out personal research using specialist magazines or Web sites, and always enquire about guarantees and technical support.

ADVICE ON CHOOSING A MATCH ANALYSIS SYSTEM

Hand notation systems

Most coaches and clubs have their own specific hand-based match analysis observation sheets and methods of evaluating results. It may prove difficult to learn how to use an existing manual coding system, and it is rare for scouts and coaches to use a system created for someone else's needs and purposes. However, if a coach does wish to exploit an existing manual system, then various points must be respected. For example, does it analyse exactly what is required by the coach? Is it easy to learn and use and, above all, productive in terms of time and output? How are the results processed and presented? These particular points are also relevant for computerised systems and are discussed in greater detail in the next subsection. It is perhaps wiser for match observers who wish to adopt an existing manual system to assess the system initially, then adapt and optimise it according to their own personal needs.

Computerised match analysis systems

Over the past decade, different high-tech computerised systems have appeared on the market and have been progressively adopted by top professional soccer teams in many different countries. As when purchasing any computer-related product, there are always many points to respect (see Figure 4.4).

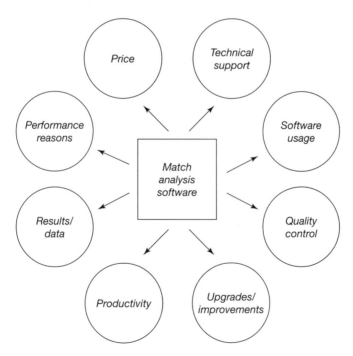

Figure 4.4 *The major factors to take into account when purchasing a computerised match analysis system*

Performance reasons

The main aim of match analysis is to provide the coach with information about team and/or individual performance. However, it is extremely important in the first place that coaches identify the reasons why they want to employ match analysis and identify exactly what they are looking for. Do they want to know who played well, who played badly, who made mistakes and suggest what needs to be improved? For example, they may have detected a particular tactical weakness within their own team performance, or the system may be used to scout the playing patterns of a future opponent. Furthermore, will the system be used mainly for tactical analysis or are motion analysis data on the physical performance of players required? Does the coach want to examine the team's defensive strategies at set-piece plays or is confirmation required that a midfield player's work-rate seemingly drops towards the end of games? If so, will further knowledge and input from a specialist defensive coach and fitness trainer be necessary? Coaches must clearly define their exact needs and what information they want out of the system. There must be a certain compatibility between their requirements and the system itself if the latter is to be of any use. Nevertheless, all computerised match analysis systems must fit the individual needs of the coach and not vice versa.

Price

The price of various systems does vary and depends of course on the type of system chosen. Even at the highest levels of the game, the club may balk at the price of a system, even though it may cost only a small percentage of a player's transfer fee or salary. The coach has to ensure that it will really be worth the outlay in terms of use and results. It is also worth enquiring whether a system can be used on a match-to-match fee basis paid to the company carrying out the analysis. This is often the case for high-tech player tracking software which involves equipping the team's stadium with accessory equipment such as videos and cameras and requires several computer operators to process the match information. Otherwise, can it be simply bought outright from a company for a one-off fee, set up and used directly by the coaching staff?

Technical support

One of the major worries with any type of purchase is, how much support will be available if there is a problem? It is extremely important that the software company offers 'after-sale' technical support in the event of any problems. Since many matches take place on evenings and weekends, technical support becomes even more significant. Is there a telephone hot-line and does this apply only during normal working hours or is there an on-site repair warranty? Does the latter involve same-day service? Does the company have an Internet site providing comprehensive information such as FAQs (frequently asked questions) or downloadable software bug fixes? Finally, does the company provide adequate software training? It is worth enquiring whether the technical support and/or training is included in the overall price. Always try to negotiate!

Software usage

One important factor to take into account is the user-friendliness of the system. Can it be learnt and used both quickly and accurately by a non-expert? What is the average time needed to learn the software? Also, it is relevant to consider whether a member of the coaching staff is to be trained to use the system, or a specialised sports scientist hired. Training by both the supplier and the club should be focused on educating the computer operator to deal with the system at every level from data input to the output of results.

A coach may like a system even though it is not optimised for his/her personal requirements. It is useful to know whether it can be personalised and adapted for individual needs. For example, the system may not include an inputting button for clearances, which may interest a coach specialising in defence. In the latest systems a new data input button may be easily created and used by the operator to analyse any preferred match action. Finally, ensure that a trial run is taken over a minimum of two or three games in order to test the overall usability of the system.

System quality control

It is essential that the overall quality of the system is high, and it must always be thoroughly assessed from start to finish. Is it robust and have there been any crashes? It is worth enquiring whether the system has been scientifically validated and thoroughly tested for stability. Furthermore, if the system is bought as a CD-ROM package, it is important to know that it will work correctly on all computer operating systems.

The end results produced by the system should be both accurate and objective. If an outside company actually undertakes the game processing using its own team of match analysts, make sure that the work is compatible with your standards. Also, are the company's match criteria or definitions satisfactory? For example, coaches may have their own definition of what is a successful action for match factors such as attacking moves. For any system, discussion should take place to agree on the criteria to be used. The end-user must be trained on what information to observe, where to look, how to look and what to look for in the results in order to avoid any possible misinterpretation.

As has already been mentioned, one major limitation of many match analysis systems is the loss of information due to replays, if using a match recording from the TV. Such gaps must be taken into account. The system may also be affected by external factors such as the environment. For example, the latest player tracking systems may experience problems resulting from poor weather conditions (see Chapter 3 for more information on computerised match analysis systems). Finally, is there an error management program to go back and correct input if an operator enters the wrong ball position, mistakes a player or misinterprets an action? Try out the system over two to three games for thorough testing and validation.

Future upgrades or improvements

Many traditional software companies offer upgrades and ongoing improvements to their products. Are these available for the desired match analysis system and is there a fee?

Also, it is important to know how these upgrades can be obtained. It is worth asking whether a company's Web site offers the possibility of downloading and installing these so-called patches. Software improvements or future versions should be negotiated at the time of purchase.

Productivity (time needed to analyse matches)

One of the major stumbling blocks with match analysis systems over the years is the time required to analyse a game. A coach may want immediate access to data during the half-time break to confirm his/her thoughts on a particular problem, or immediately after the match so that he or she can begin preparations for the following game in two or three days' time. Therefore, what is the time required to process a whole game and provide the results? Is real-time analysis possible during the live game or is the system limited to post-match analysis using a match video cassette? Depending on the coach's personal needs, the system must supply the information on demand, and productivity is the key.

Data/results

The key factors in improving performance through using match analysis are the actual data generated by the system and their presentation. Therefore, much time and care should be taken when evaluating this element of the system.

1   *Data type and relevance*: What type of data can be produced and are these relevant to what is needed for improving performance? For example, a fitness coach will be interested in motion analysis data, whereas the assistant manager may prefer a detailed tactical and technical evaluation. Also, is the manager more interested in examining the video recording rather than pure statistics? Modern systems generally offer the possibility of preparing a special video of the key match actions (video editing) linked to a digital time code. This allows immediate and time-saving access to visualise any particular moment in the game. Match video editing should now be an integral part of any system.
2   *Data quality and quantity*: As mentioned earlier, the quality of the data is vital, and this has to be checked. Also, having too many data can lead to confusion and hamper the interpretation, hence optimal use of the system is not possible. Take care that the data provided are as required.
3   *Presentation*: Coaches often judge game analysis only on output. Is there any provision for graphical data presentation and can the graphs be printed out? Also, are these data informative and easy to read and understand? Endless lists of raw data are extremely time-consuming to analyse and their potential may not be fully utilised. Furthermore, they must be presented in a clear, concise way and provide information which is straight to the point as agreed with the coach. This becomes especially important if the results are to be presented to the players. Detailed information on how to present data is presented in chapter 5.
4   *Database*: Trend analysis may be classed as being one of the most important factors in evaluating performance. Providing information over several matches or a whole season allows the ups and downs or consistency of match performance to be better

understood. For example, analysis of matches over a season may involve looking at variations in the high-intensity efforts of a midfielder or the number of free kicks conceded by a defender. Therefore, does the system include a database to allow trend analysis? If so, are the results automatically archived after each match and can they be easily retrieved for future comparisons? If this is not the case, where are the data for each game stored and how can previous performances be compared?

SUMMARY

Important factors involved in preparing and carrying out match analysis are examined in this chapter. The main take-home messages are that ample system learning time, meticulous pre-match organisation and preparation, and methodical 'live' analysis methods are needed in order to achieve effective data collection. Choosing the right equipment to observe and analyse soccer performance is never straightforward. Technology such as audio-visual and computer software and hardware is ever improving. However, price and quality can and often do vary quite dramatically. From the outset, any match analyst should clearly determine exact personal needs and available budget. These should then be compared against what is available on the market. Getting specialised advice is often a must before making any decision about purchase. Remember, only tailored, good-quality and well-exploited match analysis systems and equipment can provide a sound basis on which to analyse, evaluate and better understand performance.

CHAPTER FIVE

▼ **ANALYSIS AND PRESENTATION OF THE RESULTS**

INTRODUCTION

In the application of match analysis in training and match play, an important step in the analysis process is the presentation of results. Most coaches do not have hours to spend sifting through and trying to understand large amounts of information, and unfortunately problems do often occur. Therefore, the choice and presentation of results are highly important. Once the coach has the information required, this needs to be presented to players either individually or during team talks in the most interesting and beneficial way. This chapter concentrates on ways of looking at and analysing data, and offers advice on different presentation formats and on what and how to present during team talks, information that is gleaned from match analysis. Suggestions are also given on how to avoid potential problems when evaluating results.

LOOKING AT THE RESULTS

It is extremely important that coaches know why they want to use match analysis and what exactly they are looking for in the results. Chapter 1 describes the four major aspects of performance which can be evaluated through match analysis: technical, tactical, physical and behavioural. These sub-areas can then be broken down into whether the team is in possession (attacking play) or not in possession (defending play or 'off the ball'). This differentiation is important in evaluating the respective contributions of players in both attack and defence. For example, an analysis of the work-rate of a midfielder may confirm the viewpoint that the player is not working as hard in defence as attack.

There are various ways of analysing the match analysis data. The coach may want to look at variations or, conversely, consistency over several matches – for example, the uniformity of the physical performance of a midfield player as regards the number of high-intensity efforts over ten matches. The data may show that the player's performance is declining over this period and therefore may suggest that he/she is in need of a rest or is even carrying an injury. The various errors (e.g. dropped crosses by the goalkeeper) or examples of good performance (caught crosses) may be analysed, or performance accuracy for actions such as passing by a midfielder could be examined. Performance efficiency may also be placed under scrutiny – for example, the ratio of shots to goals by a striker. Finally, it is also possible to evaluate effectiveness. A manager who has changed the attacking style of his/her team (the ball is now played up more quickly to the strikers) may measure effectiveness over a ten-match period through the number of goals scored or attempts on goal using the new playing style compared to the previous way of playing.

As well as the different ways of analysing quantitative data, there are also various ways of examining performance in terms of player and team (own or opposition), time and according to match type. These ways may be listed as follows:

- individual analysis (single player such as a centre-forward);
- 'head-to-head' analysis (comparison of two players, such as two midfielders);
- team unit analysis (midfield, defence, attack);
- team analysis (own team, opposition);
- analysis during different periods in the game (every 3, 5 or 15 minutes);
- analysis between match halves;
- analysis over several matches;
- analysis over a whole season or several seasons;
- match type (friendly, league or cup performances).

Data may be presented under various formats such as time (e.g. total time spent in possession in opponents' half), distance (e.g. total distance run), speed (e.g. maximum sprinting speed), totals (e.g. total number of corners won), percentages (e.g. percentage of heading duels lost), ratios (e.g. ratio of on target to off target shots) and scores (e.g. match result).

It is always important to analyse data in relation to the opponents' data, to the standard of play or opposition, previous match performances and, if possible, to normative or expected data (defined from previous performance) for both individuals and teams. In addition, current form needs to be taken into account and any external factors such as the weather which could have affected the performance. These external factors are looked at later in the chapter.

With the advent of modern computerised systems, there are now several different methods available for analysing playing performance, whether quantitatively (performance data) or qualitatively (edited video recordings and game reconstructions). Both these approaches have their relative merits and disadvantages. Quantitative information is extremely useful in helping the coach make correctly informed and unbiased decisions about match performance. However, this type of information does have certain limits and may not tell the true story compared to what can be judged qualitatively on the video recording (more information on avoiding problems in data evaluation is provided at the end of this chapter). A combination of both quantitative and qualitative information may prove the most beneficial and remove any doubts resulting from using the results of only one type of analysis. A coach should always be looking to use both approaches (if possible) for information on performance in order to optimise its use in adapting future practice and training. All methods of data analysis are presented in Figure 5.1 and are described individually later in the chapter.

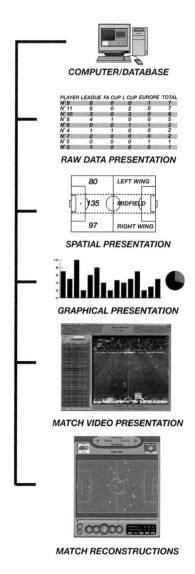

Figure 5.1 *The five major forms of presentation of the information obtained from match analysis. This information can be stored in a database*

COMPUTER GRAPHICS

As mentioned earlier, there are different ways of presenting the quantitative data obtained from match analysis. Most computerised match analysis software now provides automatic graphical output, either on-screen or by way of printouts. It is important to note, however, that the following examples of presenting results can also be created with software such as Microsoft Excel or specialised drawing packages such as Adobe Illustrator. Unfortunately, creating them may require much time and effort, especially for those who have less knowledge of information technology. It is also important to note that the graphical output discussed in this section is primarily for use by the coach and support personnel. If it is distributed to players, time and care to provide relevant explanations are needed.

Data tables

Tables of *raw* data are often time-consuming to read and it may prove difficult to extract the necessary information. As mentioned earlier, it may be useful to provide a basic match summary including attacking and defending information on tactical, technical and physical aspects. These observations can help confirm or disprove the coach's initial thoughts and feelings on the match. Further information can then be demanded on those important areas that need validating. Figure 5.2 provides a general performance summary in tabular form. The coach can quickly scan through the results and, if required, ask for more detailed information on any particular performance factor. Here, for example, more information may be required on the low percentage of shots on target or the high number of fouls committed. The coach will need to know whether the problem is, for example, physical, technical or tactical in nature. This information could be confirmed by combining the statistics with the video recording. In Chapter 4 the importance of noting any points which could affect the results when analysing performance is discussed. In this game the player was injured for five minutes and this probably had an impact on his physical performance, which was generally inferior in the second half compared to the first. This decline is reflected in terms of distance run and sprints performed. The coach can therefore take this information into account when evaluating the results. It is important to note that however good the presentation summary might be, the analyst should continually seek to improve it.

Tables 5.1, 5.2 and 5.3 present three more examples providing different levels of clarity. The first table presents similar information to that previously presented in Figure 5.2 on the attacking play of the right-midfielder. This presentation format is perhaps even easier to organise and is more pleasant to read. The second table (Table 5.2) also allows an easy comparison of tackles made across players. The reader will tend to read the information from the top down to the bottom, hence getting the correct order of data presentation is essential. The player with the most tackles is placed at the top. The third type of presentation (Table 5.3) is more difficult to read, yet provides interesting information on passing patterns between midfield players. This type of analysis is useful when analysing the playing patterns of an opposition team to know 'who passes to whom'. The most important score (passes from player no. 10 to no. 9) is presented in a slightly larger font size to attract the reader's attention to this particular bit of information. Likewise, using

Individual Player Analysis

Player: *Bob Jones*   Playing Position: *Right-Midfield*

Match: *v Team B (Youth League)*   Date: *02 January 2004*

Time played: *90 minutes*   Cards received: *Yellow*

Technical/Tactical Defending Performance:

Actions	Total	% Success rate
Tackles	10	80%
Heading duels	4	75 %
Interceptions	7	
Clearances	3	
Free kicks conceded	7	

Technical/Tactical Attacking Performance:

Actions	Total	% Success rate
Shots:	5	20%
Goal assists:	0	
Crosses:	1	100%
Passes:	26	42%
Dribbles/runs:	4	75%
Free kicks won:	1	

Physical Performance:

Actions	1st Half	2nd Half	Total
Distance run (km):	6.2	5.6	11.8
Average speed (km/h):	7.8	7.2	7.5
No. of sprints:	48	37	85
Average sprint Recovery time (s)	77	87	82

Other observations: Was off the field injured for 5 minutes towards end of second half. Came back on for end of match.

Figure 5.2 *General summary of the match performance of an individual player*

Table 5.1 *Simple attacking analysis for a midfield player*

No. 8 Right-Midfield

Total shots	10
Shots on target	5
% Shots on target	50
Goal assists	2
Crosses made	6
Fouls won	6

Table 5.2 *Comparison of the number of tackles made between the first ten and the second ten games of a season*

	First 10 games	Second 10 games
Player no. 8	32	28
Player no. 3	28	19
Player no. 5	15	16
Player no. 7	12	13
Player no. 4	9	6
Player no. 2	9	8
Player no. 6	7	5
Player no. 9	6	3
Player no. 11	4	8

Table 5.3 *Analysis of passing patterns between midfield players*

From \ To	No. 8	No. 9	No. 10	No. 11	No. 7	TOTAL
No. 8	■	4	2	3	2	11
No. 9	2	■	3	2	1	8
No. 10	4	6	■	2	1	13
No. 11	3	2	1	■	4	10
No. 7	2	1	0	3	■	6
TOTAL	11	12	6	12	11	■

different colours, or underlining particularly important results, allows quick and easy uptake of the essential information. Another way of presenting and evaluating player performance is through the creation of a success/failure index (+1 point for successful action and −1 point for unsuccessful actions) whereby the player's performance is simply indicated by a number. This possibility is discussed in more detail in Chapter 2.

Graphical information

Graphs generally allow straightforward comparison and comprehension of any match performance data. The line-graph format presented in Figure 5.3 is useful for trend analysis or the evolution of performance. This example is helpful when comparing data over time periods (e.g. every 5 minutes of a match) or over several games. This first example (Figure 5.3) allows the coach to compare the number of shots taken by the team per match over fifteen matches. It is clear that between games 6 and 9, the team was much less productive before seemingly getting its creativity back. Likewise, two-dimensional histograms are helpful when comparing various sets of data.

The second example (Figure 5.4) analyses distances run by five midfielders. This approach is useful, as an easy comparison can be made between the five players. Some computerised systems may show the results as a 'top 5' or '10'. This instantly gives the coach essential information on who ran or tackled the most, or who won the most free kicks or headers.

The next example (Figure 5.5) is concerned with shooting by a youth player. From the statistics the coach noticed that after three games, the player was no longer hitting the target when shooting. The coach decided to put into place intensive shooting practices, and the following two games clearly indicate a marked improvement in performance.

The next bar chart (Figure 5.6) simply and clearly compares various aspects of attacking play of two opposing wingers. The bars and numbers allow a quick and easy comparison of who was the more successful in each aspect of match play.

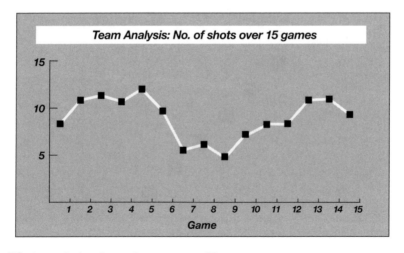

Figure 5.3 *A team's shooting performance over fifteen games*

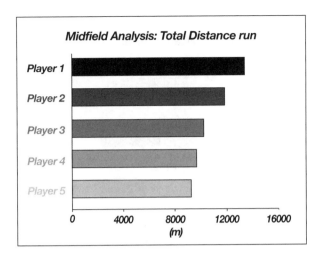

Figure 5.4 *Comparison of the total distance run by five midfielders*

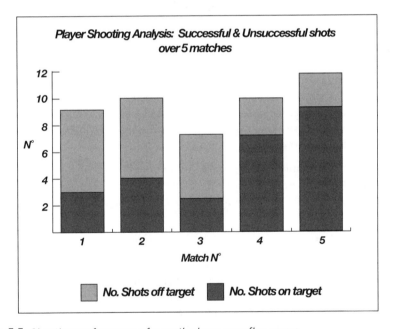

Figure 5.5 *Shooting performance of a youth player over five games*

Figure 5.7 shows the relationship between time in possession and number of shots created (represented by footballs). It is apparent that Team 1 generally dominated throughout the match (64 per cent against 36 per cent ball possession) and seemed to turn possession into scoring chances. However, this particular international match finished 3-3, demonstrating that the quantity of the criteria (Team 1 had more possession and shots) does

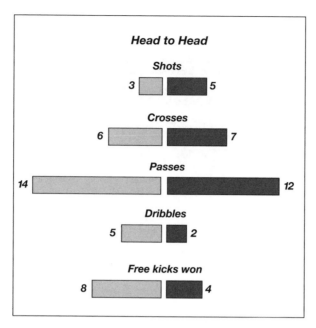

Figure 5.6 *Comparison of the attacking performances of two wingers*

not always translate into quality (Team 2 had better shots to goals ratio). It is also important to mention that problems may occur through the use of a three-dimensional histogram format featuring various sets of data, owing to the fact that bars of low-frequency data are often hidden behind those of high-frequency data. The analyst should always be careful when using this particular format.

Finally, pie charts are familiar in data analyses and are excellent for comparing percentages. In the example shown in Figure 5.8, ball possession per team per half is analysed. It is easy to see that Team B dominated possession in both halves of the match.

Spatial information

Spatial information involves information presented on a schematic representation (map) of the pitch. This format is particularly useful when analysing the different pitch zones or areas used in match play. For example, spatial information can be presented as the zones covered by the player, team units (defence, midfield, attack) or the whole team. This zone coverage can be further evaluated into play with or without the ball, in defence or attack, running movements, number and type of match actions (e.g. tackles, headers, shots) and sequential on-the-ball movements (retracing an attacking move leading to a shot). It is always important to indicate the direction of play in order to avoid confusion or misinterpretation.

The first example (Figure 5.9) is an analysis by a coach of a future opponent's attacking play. It can be seen that this team tended to attack through central or left areas. The second diagram (Figure 5.10) looks at free kicks conceded by the other team in the same

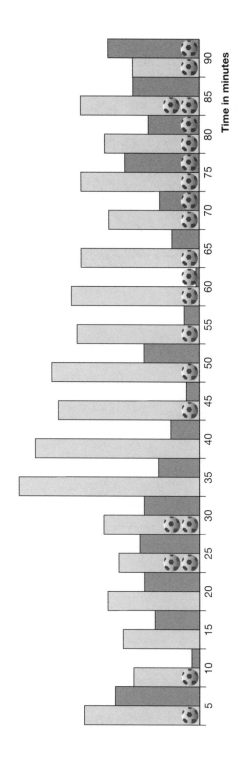

Figure 5.7 *Comparison of every 5 minutes of a game – ball possession and shots at goal – between two teams (courtesy of Sport-Universal Process)*

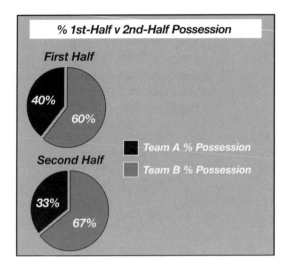

Figure 5.8 *Comparison of first- and second-half ball possession between two teams*

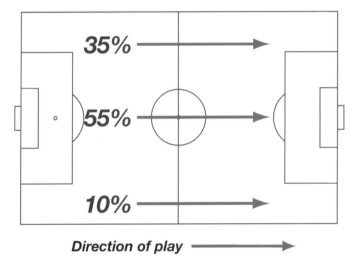

Figure 5.9 *Team attacking play examined: in which areas the team tends to attack*

game. The coach can see that this team struggled to defend against the same attacks down the left wing and conceded numerous free kicks. Figure 5.11 provides information on pitch coverage by the future opponent. The zones covered by a defender (the blacker the zone, the greater the time spent in this area) show that most of the player's time was spent in defending areas and therefore contributed little to the attacking play. The next pitch (Figure 5.12) presents information obtained from a player tracking system. The lines trace the exact movements of the player. The dark lines represent high-intensity actions.

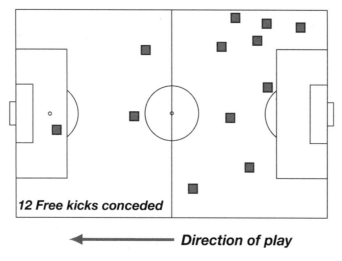

12 Free kicks conceded

← **Direction of play**

Figure 5.10 *Display showing the number and position of free kicks conceded*

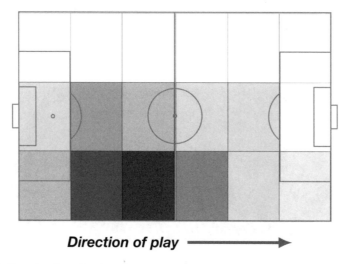

Direction of play →

Figure 5.11 *Examination of a player's zone coverage*

Figure 5.13 presents a pitch in an innovative three-dimensional layout and shows the percentage of time spent in possession of the ball. The team spent a greater amount of time in attack than defence and seemingly dominated the game. The possession of the other team in the same zones could also have been displayed to confirm or refute this assertion.

One limitation or disadvantage of using pitch maps to display information is the lack of space available. For example, a display of all 185 first-half passes of a team on a pitch

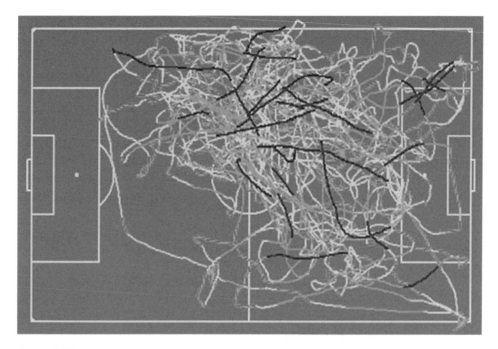

Figure 5.12 *A player's exact movements traced (courtesy of Sport-Universal Process)*

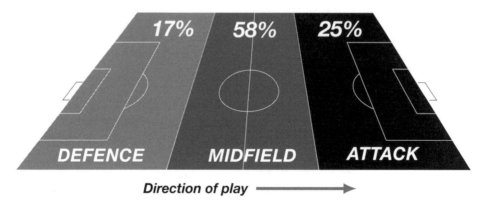

Figure 5.13 *Breakdown a team's time spent in possession in three pitch zones*

would be difficult to read or understand. However, displaying the passes which led to a shot or those intercepted in dangerous areas (such as near one's own goal) would perhaps be more useful. It is therefore essential to select and display the most essential and useful information.

Finally, Figure 5.14 evaluates the positions of on- and off-target shots by an elite French team. The number and result of the shot (e.g. save and goal) are indicated. This type of

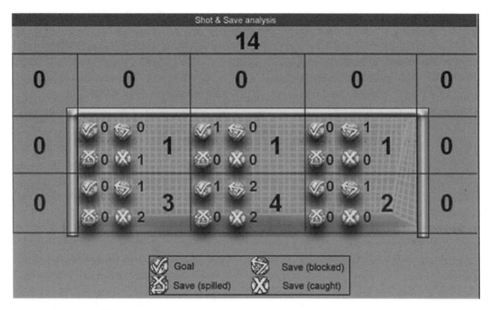

Figure 5.14 *Detailed information on the positions and outcome of a team's on- and off-target shots (courtesy of Sport-Universal Process)*

analysis can be useful for showing patterns in shooting. For example, a goalkeeper may be interested in identifying where a player tends to place the ball when taking penalties or free kicks.

QUALITATIVE INFORMATION

Video information

How video works as well as its potential are discussed in Chapter 3. Whilst quantitative data obtained from matches are extremely useful in closely analysing and evaluating the performance of players and are generally objective in nature, many coaches will tend to use match video recordings, whether those be digital (e.g. on a laptop) or analogue (using a VCR). Although a video recording provides qualitative information that may be deemed subjective in nature, most experienced coaches will generally be able to observe correctly and judge players' technical and tactical performance accurately. Physical and behavioural aspects can also be looked at and evaluated to some extent. Consequently, what type of information can the coach glean from using analysis of a match video?

The coach may simply want to look at the team performance at every set-piece play and in particular at corners and free kicks conceded. The aim is to know why the set piece was conceded, and to examine the defensive organisation when the kick was taken and the marking and pressure placed on opponents when challenging for possession. Finally, it may be interesting to know whether the team pushes out quickly after the set piece. The coach is also concerned about the defensive line-up being exposed during several attacks and will look in detail at team shape and positioning. Perhaps he or she will need to concentrate on viewing one particular defender who was often caught the wrong side of an opponent. In terms of attacking play, a closer assessment would be useful of the large number of successful moves that led to the creation of a shot by the coach's team. However, on a more negative note it seems that the two strikers are not creating enough space, and a more detailed look at their individual off-the-ball movements could be constructive. Table 5.4 presents various actions which are commonly looked at during team talks using video.

How can the coach analyse these aspects of performance through video? Perhaps the simplest method would be to watch the whole match recording from beginning to end to get an overall impression of the game. However, a coach lacking in time (often the case!) may want the club's match analyst to prepare an edited match summary or 'scrapbook' containing only the most important attacking and defensive actions. These can then be classed further into negative or positive actions such as a goal scored or ball lost by the team in question in its own defending third. The coach may have been generally satisfied with the team's performance and would prefer a detailed run-down on one particular weakness, such as the goalkeeper's handling of crosses. This may involve slow-motion, repeated close-up zooming on the keeper to analyse his/her positioning, technique and behaviour. The performance can also be analysed step by step in slow motion or freeze frame to highlight specific issues. Finally, the coach remembers one period in the match when the team was under pressure and wishes to see this particular phase again. He/she specifically may want to know the reasons why this period of pressure occurred and to see how well the team coped with it. As many modern systems combine statistics and digital video, the coach can have immediate access to lists of data on any aspect of match play. This information is often presented using a time-line with the chosen actions listed according to the time at which they took place. With the simple click of a button on an action such as a shot, the specific video clip containing the shot is immediately displayed. For example, as well as selecting, accessing and visualising the goalkeeper's performance at crosses, it is possible to click on any one shot in a list for further evaluation of the keeper's game in terms of shot-stopping. Specially prepared video highlights of a match or training may also be given to players who are injured so that they are still involved to some extent with the squad.

Table 5.4 *Basic match factors commonly looked at during team talks using video-based analysis*

Offensive actions	Defensive actions
Playing system/team shape	Playing system/team shape
Attempts on goal	Free kicks
Entries into attacking third	Corners
Build-up play	Goalkeeping
Free-kicks	One-on-one situations
Corners	Support play and denying space
Crosses	
One-on-one situations	
Support play and creating space	

Figure 5.15 *Interface of the Videosequencer analysis system developed by Sport-Universal Process to edit and visualise digital video recordings of match performance*

Match reconstructions

Every different aspect of match play can be observed and evaluated to some extent through the use of video recordings. However, the information provided is limited to what can be seen on the recording. Valuable off-the-ball information may be missed as a result of the footage concentrating on the player in possession. This problem is especially true for television coverage, although filming the game oneself can help reduce this problem to a certain extent. This lack of off-the-ball information is particularly important as players are often in possession for less than 2 per cent of the match's duration. For example, the coach may want to know why a goal was conceded from a counter-attack. Unfortunately, the footage was concentrated on the corner kick in the opposing half and therefore an analysis of the positioning of the defenders before the counter-attack started is impossible. This limitation is particularly frustrating for the coach as his/her focus was also on the attack prior to the goal being conceded. As was mentioned in Chapter 3, the development of match analysis tracking systems has helped to reduce this loss of information, especially through the development of software packages that allow the reconstruction and analysis of the exact positions, movements and actions of every player throughout the game. Whilst this player tracking has certain limitations for technical and behavioural analysis (the players are represented in a graphical format), the video can also be synchronised with and watched simultaneously with the match reconstruction to provide any missing information.

The two-dimensional representation (Figure 5.16) is especially useful for examining tactical play such as team shape or playing style. The coach can examine what every player is (or is not!) doing for the entire duration of the match. The software offers advanced match playback controls such as frame-by-frame or slow-motion visualisation. As with digital video, any particular attacking or defending action in the game can easily be chosen and immediately accessed for assessment. For example, a coach may want to look at why the team's offside trap was beaten for the first goal. Visualising the positions and movements of every player during this action makes it obvious that the opposing midfielder was not tracked from a deep central position. Also, the two central midfielders were caught out in wide positions, leaving a large gap. Similarly, the team saw little ball possession and was constantly under pressure. Through visualising his/her own team, the coach can see that the defensive players were playing too deep, therefore inviting the opposition to come towards them. This interpretation is confirmed when the coach looks closely at the time the opposition player was in possession before a defender made a challenge. The opposition was generally allowed too much time and space to build from the back. Finally, through selecting and dissecting the team's own attacking actions, it can be seen that the

Figure 5.16 *The overhead viewpoint offers a fascinating insight into, and unlimited possibilities to analyse, match performance. The Player™ software has been developed by Sport-Universal Process and is used by many top European clubs to dissect their own team's and opponents' play. The graphical line helps the coach to visualise team shape (courtesy of Sport-Universal Process).*

fullbacks tended to remain in defending positions, hence leading to a lack of width and few crossing opportunities.

USING MATCH ANALYSIS FEEDBACK DURING TEAM TALKS

Another extremely important ingredient of the match analysis process is the presentation of feedback to players on their own or opponents' performance through video footage, match reconstructions and presentation of data. These pre-planned interventions can be carried out either on an individual player-to-coach basis or during team talks. Feedback can be fitted into and presented as part of an all-year-round programme. At the end of the season the coach and staff will bring the players together to review the performance over the past year using the presentation techniques described. Before the pre-season preparation period, the coach can plan a competitive programme and set players various goals based on performance feedback from the previous season. In pre-season friendly matches the coach can analyse specific aspects of performance worked on in training to evaluate progress or identify any specific problems. This information will also allow the coach to refine different areas of match play before the season starts. Throughout the season, player and team performance can and should be evaluated at specific moments – for example, after ten matches, before and after the busy Christmas period or halfway through the season.

Team talks on a match-to-match basis centred around feedback obtained from the analysis of playing performance should also be employed. Feedback can and should be given pre-match, during the match, post-match or in the build-up to the next match. Only the coach and assistant can have the final say on the content. This feedback will probably vary according to the day of the game, past performances, the actual match performance and the final result. Information may be given before kick-off to review and recall the major tactical objectives in order to focus the team on its own performance and also to provide a few timely reminders about the opposition. It is preferable to give the talk at least two hours before kick-off since players will still be receptive to the information. Avoid introducing any new information at the last minute. It is important to remember that players are getting themselves mentally prepared for the match, and information needs to be simple and concise if it is to be assimilated correctly.

During the match, coaches will be constantly assessing team and individual performance and making tactical interventions, often based on their own opinion and sometimes on the information provided by match analysis. Some may use real-time match analysis to provide data to confirm their thoughts. For example, a coach may be unhappy about the team's attacking play at set pieces. Simple statistics may be required concerning the number of shots produced from corners and free kicks. Similarly, the coach feels that the team is being dominated, especially in midfield areas. Statistics on ball possession will either confirm or refute this opinion. However, whether at half-time or at any moment in the game, this type of information needs to be translated simply and practically, and corrective explanations provided on how to improve performance. For example, a defender may be regularly losing aerial challenges with an opponent. It may not be particularly useful to inform the player at half-time that 66 per cent of challenges have been lost. The coach will perhaps prefer to tell the player, 'You are losing most [or even, 'you have lost two-thirds'] of your headers; get closer in to the forward.' Information on performance should always be specific and relevant to the problem, and include advice on how to solve the issue.

Post-match feedback can and should be provided immediately after the game, although rash spontaneous comments must be avoided. The effective coach does not evaluate performance in a hurried or emotional manner. The feedback given may depend on the result and the coach's own opinion of both individual and team performance. The match may have been won but one player had a poor game. Does the coach therefore concentrate on the overall team performance and not the individual? Either way, feedback should be simple and practically based, with clear explanations as to how the performance could be improved. Players should always be given feedback on weaknesses and/or mistakes as well as instances of good performance. A much more detailed analysis should only take place after due time for reflection.

Many coaches prefer to give feedback the day after the match or before the next training session whilst the performance is still fresh in their own and the players' memories. This also allows more time to dissect the performance thoroughly and to prepare and present responses, in conjunction with the objectivity of the match analysis results. The major points highlighted straight after the previous game can be used to provide the structure of the team talk. This is an important occasion on which to concentrate on giving feedback in a positive manner through the use of video, statistics or match reconstructions. It is important that any criticism is constructive in nature. Players are often extremely sensitive to criticism of their own performance, even if this is presented in a constructive manner. Players may also feel threatened when their play is under the microscope, especially if various examples of weaknesses or errors are repeatedly shown. The latest player tracking systems are sometimes referred to as 'Big Brother' by players, owing to the measurement of the performance of every player during every second of the game. The information these systems provide should always be used sensitively. The coach can avoid underlining individual mistakes or problems by looking globally at the relative contributions of groups of players such as the defensive unit. Finding the right balance when identifying and presenting good performance and poor performance is essential. The match information should also be the factor that provides the context for the future training session which aims to correct or improve play. The coach should perhaps present, using video footage, an example of a certain tactical action where a problem occurred and inform the players that the next training session will incorporate and concentrate on this particular tactic. Coaches should introduce and discuss tactics as early as possible.

Feedback by means of video and match analysis can help motivate players by showing areas of improvement or perhaps the general progression in their standard of play over a series of matches. For example, a pre-rehearsed free kick routine much practised in training led to the winning goal and can be shown in detail to demonstrate how training can be rewarding. Video analysis will also enrich understanding through using real-life examples of match play to relive the experience, and allows players to understand where they are making mistakes. In addition, players who disagree with the coach's view of their performance may be proved wrong through a more detailed analysis. This situation must be dealt with delicately, as players can then feel alienated.

After the review of the previous match, it is important to present, analyse and talk about the next opponents. This area is surprisingly often overlooked, with coaches preferring to focus on their team's recent performances rather than those of the forthcoming opponents. Why is focusing on the opponents so important? First, detailed information from match analysis of the opposing team's characteristics can allow the coach to set up realistic match situations to prepare for the opposition's particular style of play and tactics such as set-piece plays. Various strengths and weaknesses will be highlighted and special attention paid to how they can be countered or exploited. Players can also feel much more confident knowing what they are about to face. The coach may want to talk about factors such as the match atmosphere if playing away, to prepare the team mentally.

Some coaches may prefer not to worry about the opposition and concentrate on their own team's performance. They may feel that building up the opponents is particularly dangerous and that no attention should be paid to them. It may not be necessary to dissect the opposition thoroughly. Likewise, showing too many mistakes or weaknesses can lead to complacency about the strength of the opposition. Pinpointing only the major factors which will help one's own team's performance when defending and attacking may prove more beneficial. The information available from observing opposition teams should never be overestimated or taken for granted. The tactics of the opponent can suddenly be changed or new players introduced which will interfere with any strategy or tactics based on observation and analysis.

An example of a team talk based around match analysis is provided at the end of this section.

The match review or analysis of an opponent can be carried out using any of the methods mentioned earlier in the chapter. Video in particular and/or match reconstructions are perhaps the best means of presenting and evaluating performance. Players generally feel more at home watching video footage. Giving groups of players detailed sheets of match statistics might not be particularly useful, as the players may not read them or may find them threatening. The coach can find it more beneficial to summarise the findings through simple comments such as 'They had most of the possession, the majority of our corners were intercepted, the work-rate of our midfield dropped in the second half . . .' The coach may find it more beneficial to use statistics on a one-to-one basis.

Finally, the coach or match analyst must always take into account and adapt presentations to the situation and the players in hand. In order to prepare and deliver powerful and effective presentations for the team talk, there are generally several points to respect:

1   Beforehand, check on how the room will be arranged, how large it is, where the analyst/coach will be positioned, the lighting, how the audience will be organised. Check that the audience can see clearly.
2   Make sure that the computer and video equipment is working and that the operator is confident in using it. There is always a risk of losing credibility if time is lost through trying to sort out operational problems. Also, make sure the players are familiar with the technological approach and methods being adopted. Players who watch a match reconstruction projected onto a large video screen may struggle to understand why and what information they are supposed to be looking at.

3   If designing multimedia presentations using software such as PowerPoint, be careful about incorporating too many special effects. Too many embellishments can actually damage the clarity of the presentation. Use appropriate transitions and special effects, such as when introducing a different part of the presentation or to highlight an important point.

4   Concentrate on verbal delivery by looking directly at the players, speaking to them rather than the computer or video screen and using good body posture.

5   Decide well ahead on the content, what will be said and what tools are needed to convey your message (e.g. video, images, graphs, game reconstructions). Remember, an image may be worth a thousand words. Until they can actually see the point in question on screen, some players may struggle to understand what the match analyst is trying to put across. Give a brief introduction on what the talk is about and a brief summary or conclusion at the end.

6   Present information in a simple way and never overburden players with complex terminology or graphical output that is too complicated. Make sure the information is adequate, relevant and accurate. Only after careful selection, analysis, validation and evaluation should match performance results be presented to players. Otherwise, the analysis and analysis methods will not convince anyone.

7   Work methodically and logically and avoid constantly changing from one topic to another. For example, work all the way through defensive analysis before moving on to attacking play. Both can be summarised together at the end of the presentation.

8   The time spent analysing games and performance must be limited. Players may rapidly lose interest and be less alert and attentive if they feel that much of what is being described does not concern them. Make sure all players feel they are concerned, and do not drag the presentation out. Players do not have to watch the whole game. A selection of the most interesting and useful moments is preferable. Professional players can be given a video recording on cassette or CD-ROM or DVD on selected key footage involving their own performance. In this way, they may learn more, as the recording contains information which is only relevant and essential to their own play. The player can also watch this copy privately without the uncomfortable presence of team-mates.

9   Adapt the presentation to the audience (i.e. age and ability) and to the situation. For example, a presentation which concentrates on motivating players through instances of good performance may be preferable if the team has just suffered a heavy loss.

10   Always encourage players to ask questions or to stop the presentation to clarify a certain point if they have not understood or need confirmation. There must always be an exchange of views between the players and the coach. Players can also be encouraged to evaluate their own performance, though some may prefer to do this on an individual basis.

TEAM-TALK SCENARIO

This example provides a practical example of a team talk based around the analysis of an opponent.

Situation

A team will play an important international qualifying match away from home. The club's match analyst is sent to watch and analyse the opposition play live at home. The match analyst is also in charge of preparing an edited video sequence using recorded footage showing the opposition's tactical and technical strengths and weaknesses. The team manager is especially concerned about the ability of the opposition to create chances and score goals. In the team's last two international matches, several goals were scored but also two were conceded. Having read various press reports, the manager is also interested in having a closer look at various individuals within the team as well as its set-piece plays.

Feedback

The match analyst provides qualitative feedback on the opponent (known as 'the opposition') to the players in the presence of the manager. This feedback contains both performance errors and examples of successful actions from both a defending and an attacking point of view. The match analyst verbally presents the different analysis points mentioned in this chapter, which are also projected onto a large screen. Each particular point is directly linked to one or more short video recordings of a corresponding match action. The team watches the action in normal speed before freeze-frame and slow motion are used to highlight certain points. The match analyst aims to present both the opposition's strengths and their weaknesses in the best possible manner. The aim is to avoid making the team feel it will be either too easy or too difficult. The following points are presented to the players:

Playing system

Use a 4-4-2 system but revert to 4-5-1 when possession is lost.

Defensive summary

- The opposition goalkeeper is strong in the air but weaker in one-on-one situations (does not close down players or angles quickly enough, also beaten twice by shots at the near post). Tends to parry shots and crosses.
- The opposition tend to defend deep and let opponents build up play. They tend not to use the offside trap.
- The midfield is often crowded, especially in central areas. Often two midfielders simultaneously challenge the same player.

- Attackers put no real pressure on opposing defenders in possession.
- Central defenders prefer to deal with high passes and have good strength in the air. They often dive in for the ball, lack pace and can be turned easily. Also, they were caught out a couple of times by counter-attacks when pushing up for corners.
- The right fullback is a good marker but is slow and lacks height, therefore is often beaten in the air. The left-back is very strong defensively.
- The opposition play a zonal defensive system which is generally well organised through good positioning and communication.
- They defend well against set pieces but tend to struggle when the ball is played on the ground.

Attacking summary

- The goalkeeper tends to play the ball out long, as do the central defenders.
- Despite the long passes, the opposition is dangerous in central areas and both midfield and forwards are comfortable on the ball.
- The forwards are often successful in winning and maintaining possession from the long passes. They often switch their positions but tend to stay in central areas.
- The midfield get forward in numbers but fullbacks are weak offensively.
- Forwards and central defenders are extremely dangerous at set pieces owing to their strong heading ability and the good ball delivery.
- Both centre-halves push up for corners and free kicks and are extremely aggressive. They have various pre-planned attacking moves.
- A significant number of headed goals are scored from corners and free kicks.
- They can quickly and successfully switch from defence to attack, especially using the long ball.

The manager then describes the various tactics to be employed and respected in order to optimise the chance of winning. These are as follows:

Defending

- Restrict the number of set pieces conceded.
- Show strict defensive organisation and discipline, and be first to the ball during set pieces. Decide who marks who. The goalkeeper must be decisive when coming for and claiming the ball. Defenders must learn and be ready to oppose pre-planned set-piece moves.
- Put pressure on the opposition goalkeeper and defenders when playing the ball long to reduce accuracy and the chance of finding the two centre-forwards.
- Try to crowd the midfield and force the opposition into using the fullbacks, who lack attacking skills. This may be achieved by the centre-forwards dropping back into midfield when the opposition is in possession in these areas. The

midfielders can also adopt a narrow triangular formation to leave more space near the wing areas.

■ Restrict and avoid getting caught out through counter-attacks. The opposition tend to invite teams forward but on regaining possession will move the ball forward at pace.

Attacking

■ Avoid high balls into the box; prefer low crosses and cutbacks. As the keeper tends to parry, follow all shots in.
■ Prefer to play down the wings; target the right-back by getting two-on-one. Own fullbacks must contribute to the attack.
■ If long balls are played from the back, hit them at the right-back, who is weak in the air.
■ We will probably have time to build up play, owing to a lack of pressing by the opposition. We can also use this to take the 'sting' out of the game.
■ When building up play near the opponent's goal, target the centre-halves by playing short, incisive passes into feet or behind the defence for attackers spinning off their markers.
■ Look to play in the gaps and for one–twos with supporting midfielders coming from deep positions.
■ As the opposition retreat quickly and in numbers when possession is lost, look immediately to catch the defence out with fast and decisive counter-attacking play.

Finally, the manager and observer answer various questions about aspects of the game. Each player goes home with a short cassette to be viewed in his/her own time on the performance of the opposing team and his/her direct individual opponent as well as a copy of the observer's match report. At the end of the session, the manager also presents the week's training content and how it will be planned. The sessions will be based on the above match analysis and will aim to counter the strengths and exploit the weaknesses of the opposition. Three major sessions will be implemented:

■ rapidly turning defence into attack;
■ breaking down a team defending in numbers;
■ defending at set pieces against a team with strong aerial ability.

AVOIDING POTENTIAL PITFALLS WITH THE ANALYSIS AND EVALUATION OF RESULTS

Any coach or member of the technical staff must dedicate ample time and energy to the analysis of results before putting the findings into practice on the training field. Some may hire a professional match analyst or sports scientist to help, but the coach is usually the one to decide what particular information is required. Nevertheless, problems may occur due to:

- a general lack of time to look properly for relevant information;
- not having the results available in time for the next match;
- restrictions or disagreements on the specific match criteria or definitions of game actions;
- difficulty or misinterpretations in understanding the results;
- inadequate, too many, irrelevant, inaccurate or poorly presented results.

The above points are extremely important and must be overcome if the credibility of the system and results are not to be questioned. For example, a common problem is defining what is meant by a successful attack. An analyst may define a successful attacking action as one which results in a shot, whereas another may consider an attack to be successful if a corner is won. In the latter case, the attacking play of a team winning fifteen corners but not scoring a goal is classed as positive. Some degree of consistency in the definition of match criteria is necessary if the coach is to steer clear of misunderstandings. Similarly, problems can occur if there are discrepancies within the results which can be pointed out by players. Some match analysts have unfortunately been known to misidentify players and mix up data.

Misinterpretation of data unfortunately can also occur. Interpretation and opinion can and often do vary between the sports scientist, match analyst, coach and the players! A player who has an 80 per cent success rate in passing may be considered much more successful than a team-mate who has a 50 per cent success rate. A closer look may show that the majority of the passes by the 'more successful' player were short and either sideways or backwards. In contrast, the other player tended to look for the more risky penetrating pass and provided the pass for the winning goal. Likewise, a player who covers less distance during the match than others playing in a similar position may do so only because of the tactics employed by the coach (e.g. a midfielder playing a 'holding' role will make fewer forward runs than players in other midfield roles). Quantity is never synonymous with quality. Pure statistical data may be misleading and not reflect the true picture of match performance. A coach may see or judge from the tables of raw data that a player had a *statistically* poor game from a tactical point of view. The coach may want to analyse the performance qualitatively through the match video and may judge that the player nevertheless put a great amount of effort into the match performance.

The way data are presented can also bring cause for concern. A team deemed to have put in a better attacking performance (20 shots at goal) than its opponents (6 shots) might not seem so successful when this information is presented as a percentage of shots on/off target. The less successful team actually was on target with 80 per cent of its shots (and won the game!) compared to 50 per cent for the successful team.

Coaches should also be aware that whilst databases are extremely useful in looking at trends in performance over specified time periods, care should be taken when evaluating previous data. As the game is constantly and rapidly evolving, owing to factors such as rule and equipment changes, better fitness and nutritional practices, and changes in the club's coach or playing style, previous data may no longer be relevant and more recent information will be more pertinent. Another difficulty encountered when working with databases may lie in defining the number of matches needed to create a performance model or profile. One method is to collect data over several matches and look for a certain

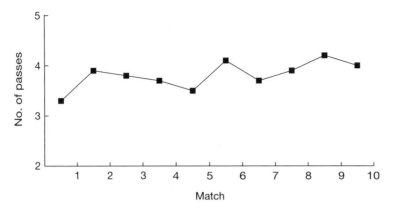

Figure 5.17 *Average number of passes per attacking action over ten games*

amount of 'stability' within the results. This is demonstrated in Figure 5.17 by analysing the playing style of a team through the average number of passes per attacking action over ten games. The graph shows that, on average, the team consistently used between three and four passes per attacking action. This profiling suggests that the team was fairly direct in its approach. Profiling other aspects of performance may, however, prove to be more difficult. Match analysis of a centre-forward's performance may show great variation in the number of shots on goal over twenty matches. In some matches the player was getting into the right positions but not receiving the ball (low number of shots) and in other games was restricted to shooting from outside the penalty area (high number of shots but lesser chance of scoring). It may be impossible to create a shooting profile for this type of player and dangerous to declare how many shots he/she should be taking each game. This shows that the type of data collected must be taken into account, as should the standard of play, since data will probably be different between amateur and professional levels.

Specialist coaches may also be needed to understand and make optimal use of certain data. For example, a specialist fitness coach is better able to evaluate and apply motion analysis data to specific training programmes. This coach may look at the close relationship between the physical capacities of players (obtained from fitness testing) and match performance. For example, the player mentioned earlier who tends to run less distance may also have a lower $V_{O2\ max}$ (maximal aerobic power), which provides a valid reason for this apparently 'inferior' performance.

Data must always be clearly laid out and easy to understand. Data may be clear to the analyst but not to others, and should be set out for the ease of the reader. The information should also be adapted to the audience and provide the right quantity and quality of relevant facts and figures. If in doubt, keep it simple and concise. In other words, avoid too much detail, but aim to keep the essentials and have more detailed data ready as back-up if necessary.

Match data can also be influenced by external factors, which can seriously affect performance. These factors are often beyond the control of the players and coach. Data on physical, tactical, technical and behavioural performance may all be concerned. These factors (listed below) should always be taken into account when evaluating performance:

Psycho-sociological factors

Playing at home seems to offer an advantage to a team, although home players may be more anxiety-prone. Increased anxiety can also affect game performance adversely. A hostile crowd atmosphere can lead to increased mental strain and bring about mistakes. Issues such as player and team motivation, confidence, concentration and the will to win all play a part in the winning or losing of games. Understanding the relationship between the mental aspects of the game and playing performance is therefore highly important. A poorly motivated player may underachieve in all competitive performance areas, whereas an over-motivated player can be a weak link as a result of poor discipline and a lack of self-control. Similarly, player confidence is essential. For example, a centre-forward may no longer be getting into decent scoring positions and may miss easy chances normally scored with ease. This is reflected by a low percentage of on-target shots.

Environment

It is well known that environmental factors play an all-important part in determining performance levels. We know that altitude, the weather and significant changes in temperature and humidity will affect performance. Moderate altitude (1.8–2.5 km) is detrimental to performance through lowering aerobic capacity and decreasing work-rate. Players may also tire earlier on waterlogged pitches than when playing on good pitches, and even simple game skills are often harder to perform on impaired surfaces. The size of a pitch is important, as teams used to large pitches may find themselves struggling to play their normal game on a smaller surface. Temperature has an influential role in affecting match play. Very hot or cold conditions will adversely affect performance. Muscle performance deteriorates as muscle temperature falls. Also, during hot and humid conditions players run less distance, sprint less frequently and are more prone to dehydration, which in turn will affect important aspects of their game.

Jet lag comes about from travelling across different time zones, and symptoms include fatigue and general tiredness, inability to sleep at night, loss of concentration, headaches and feeling sick and weak. Teams competing in games abroad may cross several time zones and will experience jet lag and have their performance impaired. The time of day also plays an important role in performance. Factors such as reaction time, isometric strength, coordination and agility as influenced by body temperature, which is closely linked to the time of day. Some players may feel less comfortable playing in the morning or around lunchtime, for example.

Player qualities

A player who can run faster and for longer, and is strong, agile and has good levels of flexibility and balance, will obviously have an advantage over the player who is weaker in any one or more of these areas. For example, a strong relationship has been found between tests of aerobic power ($V_{O2\ max}$), total distance run and the capability to repeat high-intensity efforts.

Age and gender are also important when judging and comparing performance. A 35-year-old player may not be as quick or strong as an 18-year-old counterpart but the knowledge acquired over the years may still provide a real advantage.

The interaction between the physical, technical, tactical and mental aspects of the game is fundamental. There is no point playing long passes over the defensive line-up for a slower player to run on to if this player gets beaten for pace each time. However, balls played low into the feet of the player may prove to be more successful and will lead to better individual 'statistics'. If the process of evaluating match performance data is to be fair and credible, the individual qualities of the player (whether technical, tactical, physical or mental) must be taken into account.

Other factors

The type of match to be played is important. A cup match offers different stakes as compared with a league game, and teams may have to adapt their playing styles or strategies, which will perhaps have an impact on their capacity to perform. Finally, other reasons such as luck and the decisions of the referee will always play a part in the results of a team. A bad bounce of the ball or a close refereeing decision can sometimes be the difference between success and failure.

SUMMARY

This chapter contains a detailed examination of the essential factors in the presentation and evaluation of the output from the match analysis process. It is important that problems and mistakes are avoided when studying the results, as well as ensuring that various factors which can affect performance are taken into account. It is imperative that optimal methods of data presentation are used to allow coaches to evaluate and assimilate match performance quickly and easily. Finally, the last stage in the process involves finding the best way of presenting the results during team and individual talks to ensure that future training and match performance will have fully benefited from the match analysis process.

CHAPTER SIX

▼ MOTION ANALYSIS AND CONSEQUENCES FOR TRAINING

INTRODUCTION

The major aim in using motion analysis in soccer is to obtain an indirect indication of exercise intensity. This aim is achieved by quantifying the work-rates of individual players. This information can be utilised as a reference for representing the physical aspect of each player's performance, against which work-rate profiles of other players can be compared. There is opportunity also to identify changes across matches within the same individual.

The work-rate profile indicates the gross physical contribution of a player to the total team effort. The exercise intensity during competitive soccer can be expressed as the overall distance covered which itself determines the energy used in a game. The distance covered, therefore represents a global measure of work-rate, which can be broken down into the discrete actions of an individual player for a whole game. The actions or activities can be classified according to type, intensity (or quality), duration (or distance) and frequency. The activity may be placed on a time base so that the average exercise-to-rest ratios can be calculated. These ratios can then be used in physiological studies designed to represent the demands of soccer and also in conditioning elements of the training programmes of players. The work-rate profiles can be complemented by monitoring physiological responses where possible, to provide a more complete picture for the coach.

The data obtained by means of motion analysis have implications for fitness assessment. For example, distance covered in a game is highly correlated with laboratory-based measures of aerobic power ($V_{O2\ max}$), the body's maximal ability to consume oxygen. Even clearer relationships can be established when soccer-specific tests are employed in fitness assessment. The performance profiles can highlight individual weaknesses, such as a susceptibility to fatigue, shown up as a drop-off in work-rate towards the end of a game or a need for a long recovery period after a sequence of high-intensity activities. There are direct implications for training in order that any deficiencies exposed by the analysis can be remedied.

The use of a one-off view of a particular player obtained by means of motion analysis is limited in value. In periods of lowered performance and loss of form, there may be more complex reasons for the decline than is apparent in the descriptive data. In a period of congested competitive fixtures, the work-rate profiles may give hints to help the coach's diagnosis of which players are coping well and which are failing to do so. There may be implications for the energy expenditures in training between matches, habitual activities, nutritional intake and the procedures used by the coach to aid physiological and psychological recovery strategies.

Motion analysis can help in examining the evolution of work-rates over several seasons to determine whether the physical requirements of the game are the same and whether current training programmes and fitness testing are still optimal. For example, players in the English Premiership tend to cover a greater distance during matches than did those in the old First Division. This change occurred during the 1990s. Studies of elite French players have shown that the number of high-intensity actions per match has increased by 10 per cent over the past decade. This kind of information has obvious consequences for fitness training programmes.

In this chapter the uses of motion analysis are first described. Factors affecting work-rates are then considered so that the user of motion analysis can have a better understanding of its observations. Some hints are suggested for exploring fatigue and taking remedial action. The physiological responses to match play and training are considered alongside the work-rates of participants so that motion analysis is placed within the more global context of soccer.

PRINCIPLES OF MOTION ANALYSIS

The work-rate in soccer can be expressed as distance covered in a game, since this determines the energy expenditure irrespective of the speed of movement. When a coach is utilising motion analysis, activities are coded according to intensity of movement, the main categories being walking, jogging, cruising and sprinting. Other game-related activities such as backing, jockeying for position to get in a tackle, playing the ball, and so on can also be incorporated for investigation. Tracking on paper by tracing a player's movement pathway is too prone to error and does not yield any useful information. In the early valid applications of motion analysis to professional soccer, the observer utilised a learnt map of pitch markings in conjunction with visual cues around the pitch boundaries and spoke into a tape recorder. The method of monitoring activity was checked for reliability, objectivity and validity, and is still considered to be the most appropriate way of monitoring one player per game. It requires a dedication to the task in hand, an ability to avoid being distracted by game events and technical training to keep measurement error as low as possible. For these reasons, motion analysis is best done by sports science staff rather than coaches, who nevertheless should be aware of the principles involved.

The classical method employed a subjective assessment of distance and exercise intensity recorded manually or onto an audiotape recorder. Coded commentaries of activities onto a tape recorder by a trained observer have been correlated with measurements taken from video recordings. The latter method entails establishing stride characteristics for each player according to the different exercise intensities. The data can then be translated into distances or velocities of movements. With care in conducting these procedures, the two methods are generally in good agreement, and video recordings have now replaced the classical approach. Video recording has been employed in studies of referees as well as on players during matches where heart rate can be measured throughout the game. Stride frequencies can be counted on playback of the video and these can be expressed as distance for each discrete event, provided the stride length for each activity is determined separately for the individual concerned.

A different approach to data collection is to set the activity profile alongside a time base. Categories of activity are then recorded in duration rather than in distances. This strategy permits establishment of exercise-to-rest ratios; these can be useful both in designing training drills and in interpreting physiological stresses of playing. This approach is nowadays straightforward once video systems are linked with computerised methods of handling the observations.

The various methods employed in motion analysis in soccer have incorporated ciné film of samples of individuals to encompass the whole team, overhead ciné views of the pitch for computer-linked analysis of movements, and synchronised cameras for calculation of activities using trigonometry. Hand notation methods of recording activities on paper have also been used for tabulating discrete actions, whilst computerised notation analysis, currently utilised for analysing patterns of play, has great potential for producing work-rate information. The use of six synchronised cameras linked to a computer has more recently enabled the collection of movement and behavioural information on all twenty-two players on the pitch. Whatever the method adopted, it must comply with quality control specifications. These include reliability, objectivity and validity.

A summary of overall work-rate reported in the literature (Table 6.1) indicates that outfield players should be able to cover 8–13 km during the course of a match. This activity is done more or less continuously. Although work-rate profiles are relatively consistent for individual players from game to game, the distance covered per match may vary by up to 1 km, showing that players may not always fully utilise their physical capacity. The overall distance covered during a game is only a crude measure of work-rate, owing to the frequent changes in activities. The high-intensity exercise carried out every 5 minutes is another way of analysing the overall work-rate, especially as differences between matches tend to be small. These frequent changes in activities amount to over 1,000 different movements in a game, and represent a break in the level or type of activity once every 6 seconds or so. The changes embrace alterations in pace such as accelerations and decelerations and direction of movement, execution of game skills and tracking movements of opponents (see Figure 6.1).

Table 6.1 *Mean distance covered per game, according to various sources*

Source	n	Distance covered (m)	Method
Finnish	7	7,100	TV cameras (2)
South American	18	8,638	Videotape
English	40	8,680	Tape recorder
Japanese	2	9,845	Trigonometry (2 cameras)
Swedish	10	9,800	Hand notation
Japanese	—	9,971	Trigonometry
English Premier	6	10,104	Videotape
Belgian	7	10,245	Ciné film
Danish	14	10,800	Video (24 cameras)
Swedish	9	10,900	Ciné film
Czech	1	11,500	Undisclosed
Australian	20	11,527	Video tape
Japanese	50	11,529	Trigonometry

Note: Sources of the data are cited by T. Reilly, 'Physiological aspects of soccer', *Biology of Sport,* 11: 3–20 (1994).

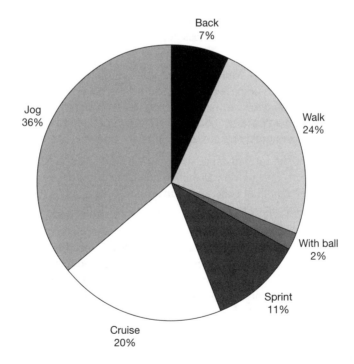

Figure 6.1 *Relative distances covered in different categories of activity for outfield players during soccer match-play. (Reprinted from T. Reilly (ed.),* Science and Soccer, *E. & F. N. Spon, London (1996) with the permission of Taylor & Francis.)*

On average, the overall distance covered by outfield players during a match consists of 24 per cent walking, 36 per cent jogging, 20 per cent cruising submaximally (striding), 22 per cent sprinting, 7 per cent moving backwards and 2 per cent moving in possession of the ball. Masked within the broad categories are sideways and diagonal movements. These figures are fairly representative of contemporary play in the English top divisions and seemingly are indicative also of other major national leagues in Europe and Japan.

The categories of 'cruising' and sprinting can be combined to represent high-intensity activity in soccer. The ratio of low- to high-intensity exercise is then estimated to be about 2.2 to 1 in terms of distance covered. In terms of time, this ratio is about 7 to 1, denoting a predominantly aerobic outlay of energy. Each outfield player on average has a short rest pause of only 3 seconds every 2 minutes, though rest breaks are longer and occur more frequently than this at lower levels of play, where players are more reluctant or less able to run to support a colleague in possession of the ball. Less than 2 per cent of the total distance covered by top players is in possession of the ball. The great majority of actions are off the ball, in running to contest possession, support team-mates, track opposing players, execute decoy runs, counter runs by marking a player, jump for the ball or tackle an opponent, or play the ball with one touch only.

During a game in top-flight competition, most activity is at a submaximal level of exertion but the importance of high-intensity efforts cannot be overemphasised. Generally, players have to run with effort (cruise) or sprint every 30 seconds and sprint all-out once every 90 seconds. The timing of these anaerobic efforts, whether the player is in possession of the ball or not, is crucial, since the success of their deployment plays a critical role in the outcome of the game.

Women's soccer seems to be played at the same relative intensity but, overall, the average distance covered is less than in the men's game. Some international female midfield players cover distances overlapping the work-rates of their male counterparts. A series of matches played by national women's teams indicate that, in comparison to men, the women take longer rest pauses, most notably before restarting the game after the ball goes out of play.

As mentioned earlier, the total distance run is only a crude measure of work-rate, owing to the frequent changes in activities. Dribbling and other activities with the ball raise the energy expenditure beyond that experienced in normal movement (see Figure 6.2), which is one of the reasons why work-rate profiles (expressed as distance covered) underestimate the actual outlay of energy in a game.

Studies in a laboratory setting have showed that energy expenditure, blood lactate and perceived exertion were elevated when dribbling was compared to running on a treadmill, the increase being similar at all four running speeds investigated (Figure 6.2). For a given speed of locomotion, the training stimulus was higher when working with the ball compared to running normally, suggesting benefits of soccer-specific work where possible. Running normally, moving backwards and moving sideways demonstrated a progressive increase in energy expenditure with increases in running speed. Since the ability to move backwards and sideways quickly is an important skill for defenders, and is itself an unorthodox movement, special attention should be given to such activities in training. Training in 'fast-feet' drills can have a beneficial effect on the short, quick movements used in close encounters with opponents.

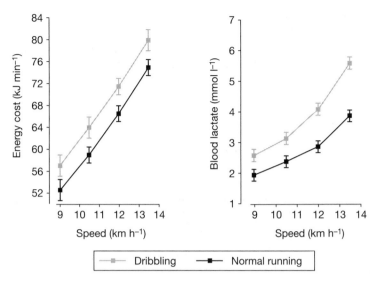

Figure 6.2 *Physiological responses to running at different speeds are higher when dribbling a ball than in normal running. (Data from T. Reilly and D. Ball, 'The net physiological cost of dribbling a soccer ball',* Research Quarterly for Exercise and Sport, *55, 267–271 (1984). Reproduced with permission from the American Alliance for Health, Physical Education, Recreation and Dance, Reston, VA 22091.)*

The dribbling elements of the game could also enhance important game skills. Dribbling capability distinguishes elite under-16 players from age-matched players at a lower level more than do shooting, passing or ball control tests. Since dribbling typically entails changes in direction to deceive an opponent, it also offers a convenient means of training agility.

It is highly unlikely that coaches will be able to implement motion analysis personally; they will need to rely on the help of the sports science support staff. Such individuals will have to detach themselves from an emotional involvement in play in order to acquire reliable data. They will also need to make preparation for conducting their analyses, nowadays employing multiple cameras. Depending on the approach adopted, they may request access to individual players to calibrate stride length at the different intensities of motion. The coach needs to help in interpreting the data generated, and so some attention is now given to describing some factors that affect work-rates.

FACTORS INFLUENCING WORK-RATE PROFILES

Positional role

A major influence on the work-rate of a player is his/her positional role. This role will depend on the overall team formation. As a group, midfield players cover the greatest distances, particularly those players who act as a link between defence and attack (as opposed to a more defensive player employed in a so-called holding role). This determinant of work-rate has been confirmed in English, Swedish and Danish league matches. Among the English league players, the full-backs showed the greatest versatility: although they covered more overall distance than the centre-backs, they covered less distance sprinting. The greatest distances covered sprinting were found in the strikers and midfield players.

The greatest overall distance was covered by the Danish midfield players, which was due to their doing more running at low speeds. This characteristic suggests an aerobic type of activity profile for the midfield players in particular. A more anaerobic type of profile is found in the centre-back and sweeper or libero. The pace of walking was found to be slower in centre-backs than for any other outfield position. The specificity of positional role is evident in that centre-backs and strikers have to jump more frequently than full-backs or midfield players. The frequency of once every 5–6 minutes confirms that while jump endurance may not be as important in soccer as in basketball and volleyball, anaerobic power output and the ability to jump well vertically are requirements for play in central defence and in attack as a 'target player'. This evidence has implications for individualising fitness training according to playing position.

Analysis has also been used to look at the relationship between physical and technical demands according to positional role and movements prior to ball contact. Data on elite English players show that forwards tend to receive the ball more frequently when cruising and sprinting than defenders and midfielders, indicating that the ability required to carry out attacking technical skills at pace is important for this position. Midfielders make more turns with the ball whilst moving than do other players, as these players must often quickly switch the point of attack in order to exploit spaces in other areas of the pitch. Defenders on the other hand make the greatest number of headers, often when sprinting.

The goalkeeper covers about 4 km during a match. Time spent standing still is much greater than for outfield players. The work-rate profile emphasises anaerobic efforts of brief duration when the goalkeeper is involved directly in play. The goalkeeper is engaged in play more than any of the outfield players, though the extent of this involvement has been reduced by the rule changes introduced in 1992 prohibiting the goalkeeper from handling the ball following a back pass from a defender. In a comparison of matches from the 1991–1992 season with the matches from 1997–1998 season, goalkeepers were less frequently involved in the 'modern game'. Passes from team-mates are now less secure and the goalkeeper needs good ball-control skills to deal with them. This rule has had only a marginal effect on the activities of outfield players. Later measures to reduce the length of rest pauses and maintain the pace of play increased the activity of outfield players (see Figure 6.3) and raised the tempo of the game.

The ability to sustain prolonged exercise relies on having a high maximal aerobic power ($V_{O2\ max}$), but the upper limit at which continuous exercise can be maintained is influenced by the so-called anaerobic threshold and a high fractional utilisation of $V_{O2\ max}$. Soccer play calls for an oxygen uptake corresponding roughly to 75 per cent of $V_{O2\ max}$, a value likely to be close to the 'anaerobic threshold' of top soccer players. Midfield players in the English leagues have higher $V_{O2\ max}$ values than players in other outfield positions. The $V_{O2\ max}$ is correlated significantly with the distance covered in a game and number of sprints made, underlining the need for a high work-rate and a high aerobic fitness level, particularly in midfield players. The distance covered in a continuous field test over

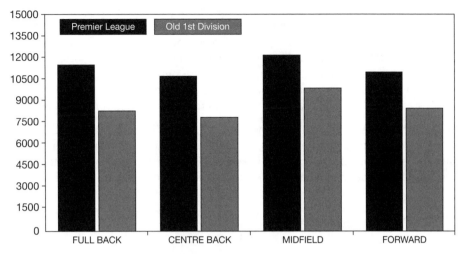

Figure 6.3 *Comparison of work-rates expressed as distance covered before and after the Premier League was established in England in 1992 (from T. Strudwick and T. Reilly, 'Work-rate profiles of elite Premier League football players',* Insight, *2(2): 28–29 (2001))*

2.16 km is also correlated with the maximal oxygen uptake. Players who do well in such a test also have a lower blood lactate concentration for a given oxygen uptake. It seems that work-rate in soccer matches depends on many of the physiological indicators of aerobic fitness found in athletes such as distance runners. This fact justifies the use of fitness testing of players and linking the fitness data to work-rate assessments. A player failing to fulfil expected work-rates in a game may (a) be experiencing a decline in aerobic fitness perhaps due to fatigue, overtraining, injury or lack of match fitness; or (b) not applying full capabilities within the game, perhaps because of the tactical choice of the coach, the tempo of the game not allowing the player to be optimally involved, or a behavioural problem such as a lack of confidence to contribute fully to the performance.

Playing style

The work-rates of players can be influenced by the style of play. Emphasis on retaining possession, slowing the pace of the game and delaying attacking moves until opportunities to penetrate defensive line-ups place emphasis on speed of movement in such critical phases of the game. Conversely, the direct method of play, a characteristic of some English clubs in the 1990s, contrasts with the more methodical build-up of offensive plays adopted by teams in Continental Europe and South America. The direct method (known also as 'Route 1'), used by the Republic of Ireland team in the 1988 European Championship and 1990 and 1994 World Cups, raises the pace of the game at all times. The main elements are faster transfer of the ball from defence to attack to create scoring opportunities, use of long passes rather than a sequence of short passes, exploitation of defensive errors, harrying opponents into mistakes when in possession of the ball and midfield players taking turns to support the strikers when on the offensive. This style of play has a levelling effect on the work-rate of outfield players since all players are expected to exercise at high intensity off the ball. A similar equalisation of aerobic fitness demands applies to the 'total football' style of play as first exhibited by the national side of the Netherlands in 1974 and characteristic of many top European club sides today. The South American style is more rhythmic and the overall distance covered in a game is about 1.5 km less than in the English Premiership. The comparison is shown in Figure 6.4, although the profile of Roberto Carlos (playing with Real Madrid at the time) representing Brazil is closer to the average for the Premier League players than for the other South Americans.

The so-called direct method tends to even out differences in work-rate between playing positions. Whilst this style of play was used by Ireland's national team in the 1990s, it evolved to accommodate individual differences. For example, players selected for the 1994 World Cup qualifying matches included some individuals known for exceptionally

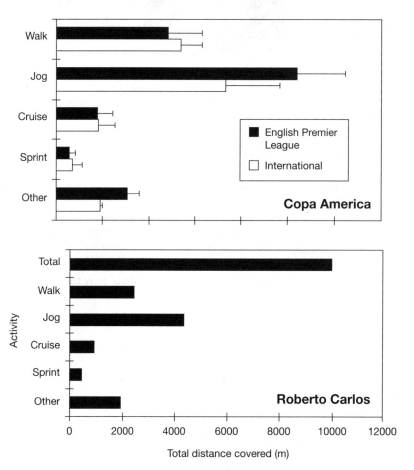

Figure 6.4 *Work-rate profiles of individual South American players at the Copa America Tournament alongside figures for the Premier League. The corresponding work-rate of Roberto Carlos while playing for Real Madrid is illustrated as a comparison. (Reprinted from* Sports Exercise and Injury, *vol. 4, B. Drust, T. Reilly and E. Rienzi, 'Analysis of work-rate in soccer', pp. 151–155', copyright 1998, with permissions from Elsevier.)*

high work-rates and one player whose training programme was habitually hampered by chronic injury. This diversity acknowledges that team managers do consider building teams around highly talented players. The direct method was also employed by Norway's and Poland's national teams during the 1990s, although in both instances this strategy probably compensated for a lack of exceptionally gifted individuals in the teams. A modification of the direct approach was employed successfully by the players from Greece in the Euro 2004 tournament, countering the possession-oriented style of more gifted teams. The 'direct method' is no longer used by competent teams as a style of play, but may be used periodically to catch unwitting opponents off guard. For example, the goalkeeper may release the ball quickly to a target striker who, on gaining possession, may drive directly at the opponent's goal.

Fatigue

Fatigue may be defined as decline in performance due to the necessity to continue performing. In soccer it is evident as a deterioration in work-rate towards the end of a game. Comparisons of the work-rate between first and second halves of matches have indicated the occurrence of fatigue. It may also be identified if activities during the game are broken up into 15-minute or 5-minute blocks.

Belgian players have been found to cover on average a distance of 444 m more in the first half than in the second half, and similarly the distance covered in the first half by Danish players was 5 per cent greater than in the second. This decrement does not necessarily occur in all players. An inverse relation between aerobic fitness ($V_{O2\ max}$) and decrement in work-rate implies that players with the higher $V_{O2\ max}$ values, those in midfield and full-back positions, show the least drop in distance covered in the second half. In contrast, centre-backs and most strikers have higher figures for the first half. It does seem that the benefits of a high aerobic fitness level are especially evident in the later stages of a match.

The total distance in sprinting is often unaffected between playing halves, and the number of high-intensity actions may even increase in the last few minutes of the game. Players tend to carry out fewer actions at low or moderate intensity, indicating that they may tend to 'spare' their efforts for the final few crucial actions as their energy levels begin to get low. A midfielder may choose to support an attack or a centre-forward help out defensively by quickly closing down space. It may be interesting to look at the distance covered, duration or the maximal speed of individual sprints to determine whether a player's sprint performance is declining. It would also be interesting to examine whether the intensity of the following sprint is affected by the intensity of the previous sprint (e.g. if the sprint is extremely long and at maximal speed). It may also be useful to look at the relation between the intensity of the activities immediately after the previous sprint (e.g. whether moderate-intensity exercise will affect ensuing sprint performance more than efforts at low intensity). Individual sprints will often depend on the requirements of the game situation, and particularly the recovery allowed by the ebb and flow of play.

Figure 6.5 presents the maximal sprint speed of an elite French midfield player averaged every 5 minutes throughout the match. The player was generally not as quick towards the end of the match as at the start. This information could lead the coach to change tactics

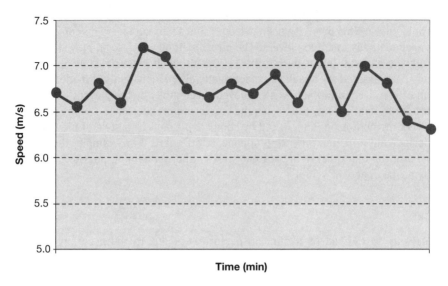

Figure 6.5 *Maximal sprint speed for a particular player averaged every 5 minutes during a game*

or even make a substitution to avoid the opposition exploiting this emerging physical weakness.

The main cause of a decline in work-rate towards the end of a game is a reduction in energy. The amount of carbohydrate stored as glycogen in the leg muscles pre-match appears to have an important protective function against fatigue. Players with sound nutritional preparation for matches tend to show a more stable work-rate profile through-out a game than do those who prepare more casually. Swedish club players with low glycogen content in the vastus lateralis (thigh) muscle were found to cover 25 per cent less overall distance than the other players. A more marked effect was noted for running speed: those with low muscle glycogen stores pre-match covered 50 per cent of the total distance walking and 15 per cent at top speed compared to 27 per cent walking and 24 per cent sprinting for players who started with high muscle glycogen concentrations. Attention to diet and maintaining muscle glycogen stores by not training too severely are recommended in the immediate build-up for competition. These considerations would be most important in deciders, where drawn matches are extended into 30 minutes of extra time and most outfield players are likely to run down their stores of carbohydrate. They also explain why players coming onto the field as substitutes towards the end of a game tend to have higher work-rates than their departed colleagues. The observations demonstrate the impact of physiological preparation and match demands on the changes in work-rate profiles that occur as the game goes on. The profile can also be stabilised by an appropriate nutritional strategy.

A fall in activity at the beginning of the second half may be due to the players getting 'cold' in the half-time break. Some players may cover more ground in low-intensity activities during the opening 15 minutes of the first half compared to the same period in the second half. This difference may be linked to a higher initial motivation and a thorough warm-up session in the first half. In contrast, during the half-time break players tend to rest, which causes a drop in muscle temperature. They return to the pitch unprepared, and sprint performance can be affected at the beginning of the second half. Undertaking a few minutes of low- to moderate-intensity exercise during the pause may help players to 'ready' themselves and to perform better physically. The optimal way of treating a 15-minute interval is for the first 7.5 minutes to be a rest whereas the remainder can be used for light activity to keep the muscles warm. This activity can be done in the dressing room or out on the pitch with the ball.

Goals may be scored at any time during a game, but a higher proportion than would be expected is scored towards the end of games. This phenomenon cannot be explained simply by a fall in work-rate, as logically this would be balanced out between the two opposing teams. A more pronounced deterioration amongst defenders would give an advantage to the attackers towards the end of a game. Alternatively, it may be linked with 'mental fatigue': lapses in concentration as a consequence of sustained physical effort leading to tactical mistakes that open up goal-scoring chances. The late surge in scoring may be a factor inherent in the game, play becoming more urgent as the end approaches despite the fall in physical capabilities. A rise in critical incidents in contesting possession of the ball occurs in the first 15 minutes and in the last 15 minutes of the game. Players seek a physical means of registering their presence on the opposition at the start, whilst near the end of the game, contests for possession may become more desperate. Irrespective of the existence of the fatigue process, a team that is physiologically and tactically prepared to last 90 minutes of intense play is the more likely to be an effective unit. Event analysis can highlight for the coach those individuals who can remain combative until the game ends as well as those who are prone to error or lapses in concentration.

The analyst may explore the observations for the coach with specific questions in mind. The coach may wish to look at two or more work-rate profiles together to see how midfield players are sharing workloads between them. There may be a focus on one particular individual at a critical time in the game to search for any evidence of buckling under pressure. The observations could also be examined to see how well players tended to support the player in possession and work off the ball. This line of analysis could be extended to the work-rates of players when defending (the opposition in possession) compared to attacking (own team in possession). This comparison may help determine whether players such as midfielders are working as hard in a defensive role as they are in attack.

Medical staff may attempt to find patterns between work-rates and injury and play a role in prediction and prevention of injuries. A decline in performance over several matches (e.g. distance run, number of sprints, and so on) may suggest that a player is in need of a rest and could be becoming susceptible to overtraining. It may also be interesting to evaluate the relationship between exercise intensity and injury to establish whether players suffer more injuries after strenuous periods of high-intensity exercise. Motion analysis could help explain why non-contact injuries occur in players and allow the coach and players to prevent a recurrence. Players returning after injury could have that profile scrutinised to see how they recovered from intense periods of play or to have their performance compared against a benchmark profile obtained from previous matches.

The environment

The environmental conditions may also impose a limit on the exercise intensity that can be maintained for the duration of a game or hasten the onset of fatigue during a match. Major tournaments – for example, the World Cup finals in Spain in 1982, in Italy in 1990, the United States in 1994 and Japan in 2002 – have been held in hot countries with ambient temperatures above 30°C. Similarly, teams touring in the off season or pre-season may visit countries where heat presents problems for them. The work-rate is adversely affected when hot conditions are combined with high humidity. Performance is influenced both by the rise in core temperature and by dehydration, and sweat production will be ineffective for losing heat when relative humidity approaches 100 per cent. Cognitive function, such as the kind of decision-making required during match play, is better maintained during 90 minutes of continuous exercise when fluid is supplied inter-mittently as compared with subjects compared to a control condition. Adequate hydration pre-exercise and during the intermissions is important when players have to play in the heat. The opportunity to acclimatise to heat prior to competing in tournaments in hot climates is an important element in the systematic preparation for such events. With an astute location of training camps, good physiological adaptation is achieved within 10–14 days of the initial exposure in hot weather, or with regular and frequent exposures to heat in an environmental chamber near to home.

The match analyst and the coach should also be aware of how performance characteristics are affected by a cold environment. Playing in cold conditions is likely to be associated with impaired work-rate and increased liability to injury. This injury risk would be pronounced when playing on icy pitches without facilities for underground heating. Muscle performance deteriorates as muscle temperature falls; therefore, a good warm-up prior to playing in cold weather and use of appropriate layers of sportswear to maintain warmth and avoid the deterioration in performance known as fatigue would be important. Injury is more likely to occur in players if their warm-up routine is inappropriate. Therefore, pre-match exercises should engage the muscle groups employed during the game, par-ticularly in executing soccer skills.

The interactions between environmental variables and soccer performance also include altitude. Soccer coaches have only infrequent experience of competing at altitude, usually in pre-season tournaments at training-camp resorts. Above an altitude of about 1.8 km, aerobic function is likely to be affected. The ability to sustain exercise at a high proportion of $V_{O2\ max}$ is likely to be impaired, whilst recovery from high-intensity exercise will be delayed. Performance with the ball may be more complicated than normal since it will fly through the less dense air more easily than at sea level. Motion analysis can help to highlight those individuals most susceptible to reduced performance at altitude by monitoring their work-rates. It could also be used in planning strategies for playing at altitude, with a view towards timing short periods in the game for recovery to take place.

There is also a possibility that the work-rate may be affected by whether the game is played at home or away. The home venue is thought to offer an advantage to a soccer team, whether this bias is due to playing in familiar surroundings or to support from a partisan crowd. Home advantage is reflected in the fact that close to two-thirds of all points gained in the English Football Leagues go to the home side, a trend that has not changed since the League was formed in 1888. The advantage of playing at home is less pronounced in local derbies, but is more marked in European Cup matches. Players are more anxious when playing before their home supporters. This effect is not reflected in overall work-rate profiles, which tend to be the same at home and away matches. Nevertheless, individuals may have spells of poor performances when their own supporters turn against them, and match analysis can help to highlight where deficiencies arise. The objective is to correct their faults, restore the confidence of the players concerned and secure a restoration of the quality of performance expected.

PHYSIOLOGICAL CONSIDERATIONS

Motion analysis can help to highlight the demands imposed by match play, but such information is most valuable if it can be linked with the physiological responses of players. In order to optimise motion analysis data, sports science personnel may need supplementary physiological information. Energy expenditure can be estimated in training contexts or friendly matches by collecting expired air for analysis of its volume and gas contents. Lightweight telemetric systems are now commercially available and have been used alongside time-and-motion analysis of training drills to establish their training intensity. Drawing blood samples from players at convenient breaks in their activity has helped to outline the metabolic and hormonal changes that occur as the game progresses. The preferred fuel for exercising muscle alters towards an increase usage of fat in order to avoid a premature depletion of liver and muscle glycogen stores. The monitoring of core body temperature has also contributed to an understanding of how excess heat stored by the body can lead to impaired performance, either directly due to overheating or indirectly due to reduced hydration status associated with sweat losses.

Blood lactate responses to exercise are used to indicate anaerobic glycolysis. The data are variable, possibly being partly a function of the timing of the sample. Values are generally not high, although concentrations approaching 10 mmol.l^{-1} may be found. Blood lactate concentrations tend to be higher at the more intense levels of competition (owing to the fact that more high-intensity exercise is carried out by elite players) and in samples obtained at the end of the first half compared to the end of the second half (Table 6.2). While lactate concentration in blood underestimates lactate produced within the muscle, it is likely that the overall anaerobic energy yield from this source during a game is small. This is because the total duration of high-intensity exercise during a match (including cruising and sprinting) accounts for only about 8 per cent of game time and the average sprint is for a distance of about 14 m. The vast majority of activities are of low to moderate intensity and engage aerobic processes. Nevertheless, crucial events in the game call for high anaerobic output of energy and these movements can be targeted by means of match analysis. If, for example, a player tends to lose out through poor acceleration or lack of speed over a short distance, the trainer should be able to suggest a remedial programme of strength and power training, or the use of so-called 'complex training'. Figure 6.6 compares the acceleration and maximal sprinting speed of a French centre-forward and a Norwegian centre-half when sprinting for a ball played into space behind the Norwegian defence. This example shows that the forward was generally 'beaten for pace' by the defender. The coach may want to implement a specialised speed training programme for

Table 6.2 *Mean (± s.d.) blood lactate concentrations (mmol.l⁻¹) during a soccer match*

First half	Second half	Source
4.9 ± 1.6	4.1 ± 1.3	Smaros (1980)
5.1 ± 1.6	3.9 ± 1.6	Rohde and Espersen (1988)
5.6 ± 2.0	4.7 ± 2.2	Gerisch et al. (1988)
4.9	4.4	Bangsbo et al. (1991)
4.4 ± 1.2	4.5 ± 2.1	Florida-James and Reilly (1995)

Sources: G. Smaros, 'Energy usage during a football match', in L. Vecchiet (ed.), *Proceedings, 1st International Congress on Sports Medicine Applied to Football*, vol. 11, D. Guanello, Rome, pp. 795–801 (1980); H. C. Rohde and T. Espersen, 'Work intensity during soccer training and match-play', in T. Reilly, A. Lees, K. Davids and W. Murphy (eds), *Science and Football*, E. & F. N. Spon, London, pp. 68–75 (1988); G. Gerisch, E. Rutemoller and K. Weber, 'Sports medical measurements of performance in soccer', in T. Reilly, A. Lees, K. Davids and W. Murphy (eds), *Science and Football*, E. & F. N. Spon, London, pp. 60–67 (1988); J. Bangsbo, L. Nørregaard and F. Thorsøe, 'Activity profile of competition soccer', *Canadian Journal of Sports Sciences*, 16: 110–116 (1991); G. Florida-James and T. Reilly, 'The physiological demands of Gaelic football', *British Journal of Sports Medicine*, 29: 41–45 (1995).

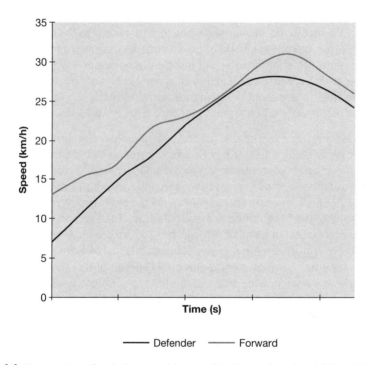

Figure 6.6 *Comparison of sprinting speed in two elite players (courtesy of Sport Universal Process)*

this player or alter tactics by playing the ball low towards his feet rather than into space for the player to run on to.

The most widely used strategy for estimating metabolic demands has been to measure heart rate during match play and juxtapose the observations on heart rate-V_{O2} regression lines determined in a laboratory during incremental running on a treadmill. This estimate could nowadays be made from a progressive test in the training grounds using telemetric devices. The estimate of V_{O2} from observations of heart rate could in theory overstate the actual O_2 consumption, owing to the factors (heat, emotional stress, static exercise) that cause heart rate but not V_{O2} to rise. The error is thought to be small, since it is only for short periods that the relation between heart rate and V_{O2} in the game differs from that obtained in laboratory conditions. The heart rate in itself provides a useful index of overall physiological strain, quite apart from its use in estimating V_{O2}.

Traditionally, long-range radio telemetry has been employed to monitor heart rate during friendly matches or simulated competitions. In recent years, the use of short-range telemetry (Sport-Tester) has been adopted. Observations generally confirm that the circulatory strain during match play is relatively high and does not fluctuate greatly during a game. The variability increases in the second half of play at sub-elite level, as the players take more rest periods. The heart rate remains above 75 per cent of the heart-rate range (maximal minus resting heart rate) for 66 per cent of the playing time. For the larger part of the remaining time, the heart rate exceeds this level.

It is feasible to analyse work rates in training as well as during competition. It is possible in a training context to monitor heart rates of all the players involved using multiple short-range telemetry systems (Team system, Polar Electro). Such recordings can yield vast amounts of data, so it is important that there is a clear purpose for the measurements. The most obvious use of such comprehensive systems is to ensure that the training stimulus is sufficient to elicit the desired response, or that it is at a level that will avoid overtraining. The exercise intensity can be expressed in 'bandwidths' corresponding to the mean heart rate of the activity engaged in. In this way the training programme may be regulated in a scientific manner.

STRATEGIES TO REDUCE FATIGUE

Once a susceptibility to fatigue is identified in individual players, the reasons for its occurrence should be explored. It may be that fatigue occurs only as the end of a game draws near. The reason can be inadequate attention to nutritional preparation for the game, or it may be that the player concerned trained too hard the day before, lowering muscle glycogen content in the process. Another possibility is that the player lacks the endurance to sustain play at the tempo required. Substituting this player before the onset of fatigue would restore balance to the team, and may even have added value. The player coming on will have 'fresh legs' and full glycogen reserves, and should have a higher work-rate capability than those who have played from the initial kick-off. The appropriate timing of the substitution of players by the coach is therefore clearly important. This timing should be underlined when the coach makes a comparison of the substitute's work-rate with that of others.

Fatigue may also be evident as a prolonged recovery during the game itself. The reason might be that the player concerned was put under pressure repeatedly by the opposition, eventually becoming unable to respond to game demands. This type of fatigue is transient, the player recovering once there is respite from the opponents. In this instance, providing tactical support for the player targeted is important so that the offence from the opponents is not relentless.

Players who are aerobically well trained can maintain their work-rates better towards the end of the game than can those of poorer aerobic fitness. Aerobic training also speeds recovery following high-intensity efforts. Active recovery at low to moderate intensity accelerates removal of lactate from the blood compared to standing still. Speed-endurance training can help players to improve their ability to perform high-intensity exercise repeatedly and may prevent them from slowing down towards the end of the game. An example of a speed endurance session based on work-rate analysis is provided at the end of the chapter.

As mentioned earlier, nutritional strategies can also be effective in decreasing the effects of fatigue. Pre-start muscle glycogen levels are influential in determining players' performances. The energy provided in sports drinks that contain glucose may delay fatigue, partly by saving muscle glycogen stores. Various studies have shown that glucose ingestion lowers the net muscle glycogen utilisation during soccer.

The benefits of carbohydrate ingestion may not be evident in the execution of soccer skills late in the game. Nevertheless, youth professional soccer players have reported positive subjective effects from consuming a maltodextrin (carbohydrate) solution during a long training session where performance decrements would otherwise be expected. Evidence for a similar effect on motor skills such as tackling, heading, dribbling and shooting during a game is not yet available.

Dehydration can contribute towards fatigue, particularly when matches are played in the heat. The positive effects of rehydration at half-time, and since the 1994 World Cup in the United States at the sidelines when breaks in play permit, have been found mainly in laboratory studies of 90 minutes' exercise, rather than in soccer matches, where conditions are more difficult to control and evaluate.

The team with the superior tactical ability can dictate the pace of the game so that the performance capabilities of outfield players are not overtaxed. Alternatively, players may share high-intensity bouts in turn so that the overall pace of play is maintained. In environments such as at altitude and in the heat, the ability to pace the total team effort economically is especially important. The coach has to be alert to the changes in work-rate that a switch in tactical role can produce and use such information to best effect.

SUMMARY

A number of approaches to the complex assessment of game demands have been employed by various groups of researchers. The reference data have been based on motion analysis of actual soccer matches. It is important that the method chosen should fit the purpose intended. The limitations of particular approaches should be appreciated for the analyst to interpret the observations correctly and for the coach to implement the findings sensibly.

The physical demands of soccer are complex and rely on the player's ability to perform prolonged intermittent exercise (endurance), at low, moderate and high intensities, show a capacity to sprint repeatedly and recover, and to develop a high power output in various match actions such as jumping or tackling. Positional role, playing style, game tactics, players' fitness levels and environmental factors will all influence work-rates. Physiological measurements can be used to complement work-rate data. Players tend to experience fatigue towards the end of the game, though this decline in performance can be offset by adapted fitness training, good nutritional habits and appropriate tactical decisions.

In view of the richness of the observations generated from motion analysis, interest in this area is likely to continue to grow. Match analysis systems have improved considerably over the past three decades since the pioneering applications of time-and-motion methods to soccer. Contemporary analytical systems range in complexity, but their value depends on establishing a clear purpose to their use. Computer-aided and digital video systems have enhanced the opportunities available to coaches to obtain reliable feedback on performance by marrying notation and motion analysis. The further development of analytical systems is inevitable. The precision and accuracy of estimating accelerations, velocities and distances could be improved by tagging players and using ultra-broadband frequencies for recording movements rather than relying on contemporary video-based methods.

MOTION ANALYSIS SCENARIO

This scenario provides a practical example of how to apply the results from motion analysis into soccer fitness sessions.

An elite centre-forward has recently returned from injury. The player's work-rates have been analysed over two comeback reserve team matches using the very latest in player tracking systems. The reserve team manager feels that the player has struggled towards the end of matches. Work-rate data show that the player is suffering from a decline in high-intensity exercise performance, especially during the last 15 minutes of the match. Analysis of these high-intensity actions shows that the player's ability to perform repeated sprints at similar high speeds with short rests and to maintain these high speeds has diminished when compared to his performance before the injury. Maximal speed and duration of sprints tend to decrease and recovery time between actions increases. Complementary notational analysis also shows that the player touched the ball less frequently towards the end of the game and that the majority of his technical actions were unsuccessful. The club's sports scientist presents the results to the fitness coach, who decides that the player is lacking in speed endurance or the ability to perform maximal or near-maximal sprints repeatedly. The fitness coach and player discuss the results and agree on a specific training programme. Over the next three weeks, the player will undertake six extra sessions (after normal training) based on 'production' work where high-intensity exercise will be carried out almost maximally for short periods of 20–40 seconds with 2–4 minutes' recovery and 'maintenance work' (see the example drill in Figure 6.7) involving almost maximal exercise of 30–90 seconds

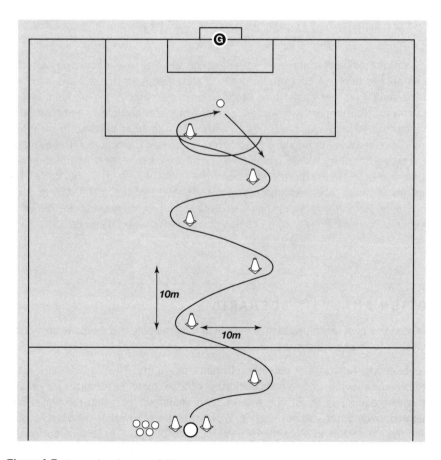

Figure 6.7 *A speed endurance drill*

with a similar or shorter recovery time. The fitness coach explains that the "production training" will aim to improve the player's ability to perform maximally for a relatively short period of time by enhancing the anaerobic processes and allowing sufficient rest to ensure full recovery between bouts to maintain a very high intensity. The maintenance training aims to increase the player's ability to sustain exercise at high intensities and improve recovery. Before commencing the extra training, the player also undertakes a field test incorporating repeated sprints and recovery periods. The fitness coach can then determine from the individual sets the best sprint time (the fastest of all the sprints), a mean time (total time of sets divided by number of sets) and a fatigue time (fastest set minus slowest set). The coach will repeat this test after the sixth session to determine how effective the training has been (e.g. lower mean and fatigue team). Finally, heart-rate measurements are employed during the training sessions to ensure that the player has adequate rest between sets and that the intensity is high enough to stimulate improvement.

Organisation

Half-pitch plus full-size goal; eight cones plus six balls (see Figure 6.7).

Description

This functional intermittent exercise drill with shots at goal involves a set of three almost maximal runs of approximately 1 minute in duration interspersed by active rest periods lasting 2 minutes before a break of 3 minutes is taken. The set of three runs is then repeated. The duration is around 20 minutes in total. On a signal the player sprints through the cones as indicated, shoots at goal, turns and sprints back again through the cones to the start. The player then recovers by gently dribbling a ball to the penalty spot and jogs back to the start before repeating the drill.

Variations

For the second and third sessions, increase the number of runs to four then five or reduce the recovery period by 30 seconds or to the same as the exercise time.

Shooting can be mixed with heading and passing actions.

Coaching points

The player must be continually encouraged during the drill. Avoid this type of session the day before a match, because of the high fatigue levels experienced. Further work-rate analysis during competitive matches should (if possible) be employed to determine the effects of the training.

CHAPTER SEVEN

▼ WHAT MATCH ANALYSIS TELLS US ABOUT SUCCESSFUL STRATEGY AND TACTICS IN SOCCER

INTRODUCTION

Successful coaches have an almost insatiable appetite for knowledge about every facet of the game. The coach's craft knowledge is developed through playing the game, observing matches and successful mentoring by more experienced coaches. Whilst this knowledge is very helpful in developing an extensive library of information relating to successful strategy and tactics, it is nevertheless subjective and potentially confounded by personal biases and expectations. Quantitative match analysis is therefore invaluable to the coach in that it can help create an objective, unbiased view of events and provide a solid platform upon which to make informed decisions as to successful strategy and tactics. In this chapter we provide a review of some of the major findings that have emerged in recent years based upon the quantitative analysis of matches. The conclusions are based mainly on a detailed analysis of matches from international tournaments over the past six years, sprinkled with some less frequent observations from the English Premiership and European Champions League. Most researchers have focused primarily on successful attacking soccer, although some implications for defensive strategy and tactics may be drawn via inference. Similarly, there would appear to be limited data on the women's game bar a few snippets from the 1999 World Cup. The majority of the research presented was undertaken by Liverpool John Moores University on behalf of the Football Association's Coaches Association with findings having been previously reported in its publication *Insight*.

THE IMPORTANCE OF SET PLAYS: PREPARATION AND PLANNING

A significant proportion of goals are scored either directly (i.e. a first-phase goal where the ball is not touched by the opposition) or indirectly (i.e. a second-phase goal where the ball is cleared and then immediately played back into the danger zone) in domestic and international soccer. When second-phase goals are considered, almost half of all goals are scored via this route. The proportion of goals scored from open play and various types of set plays in the 2002 World Cup is presented in Table 7.1. This breakdown is fairly consistent across domestic and international soccer, with free kicks being the most important, followed by corner kicks. In the 1999 Women's World Cup the four semi-finalists scored almost 58 per cent of their goals from set plays.

Table 7.1 *Source of goals in the 2002 World Cup*

	Total	%
Free kick	27	17
Corner	21	13
Throw	17	10
Penalty	13	8
Open play	83	52
Total	161	100

Frequency and productivity of set plays

In international soccer, teams have an average of 12 indirect free kicks, 2 direct free kicks, 17 throw-ins and 5 corner kicks in the attacking third per game. The overall frequency of set plays has declined slightly in recent years. This downward trend in overall set-play frequency is evident in domestic and international soccer, particularly in relation to corner kicks. The frequency of set plays in domestic soccer is generally slightly higher than in international games.

In contrast to the observed decrease in set-play frequency, there has been a significant increase in efficiency, with more goals being scored from fewer set plays. Successful teams are far more efficient than their opponents at scoring from set plays (with a typical set play to goal ratio of 1:7 for successful teams compared to 1:15 for opponents). The importance of preparation and planning at set plays is highlighted.

Why are set plays awarded?

As highlighted in Figure 7.1, in the 2002 World Cup the highest proportion of free kicks in the attacking third were awarded after a player had been fouled when running or dribbling the ball past a defender, particularly in central areas of the field. This finding highlights the importance of having players who can commit defenders to making challenges by running or dribbling with the ball in attacking areas. The majority of the remaining free kicks were awarded following fifty–fifty challenges or when players were about to receive or turn with the ball or in a 'head-on' challenge.

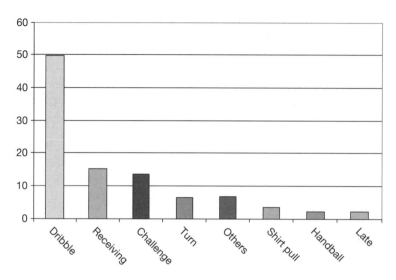

Figure 7.1 *Causes of free kicks in the attacking third in the 2002 World Cup*

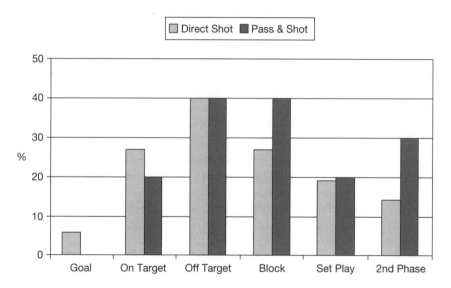

Figure 7.2 *Outcome of direct shots from free kicks in central areas within the attacking third in the 2002 World Cup*

Attacking free kicks in central areas

A breakdown of free kicks awarded in central areas in the 2002 World Cup is provided in Figure 7.2. The trends for the 2000 European Championships were very similar. A reasonable proportion (8 per cent) of goals came from direct shots in central areas. However, no goals were scored from free kicks that involved a short pass followed by a shot at goal. The latter finding may be due to defensive players quickly closing down the space between them and the ball, reflected by the high proportion (40 per cent) of blocked free kicks in this category. Also, a higher proportion of free kicks involving a direct shot hit the target compared with those involving a short pass and a shot. A direct shot at goal is far more advantageous than a pass-and-shoot strategy in central areas. There may be defensive implications for trying to make the wall look as big as possible, thereby encouraging opponents to use the 'pass-and-shoot' strategy rather than a direct shot.

Table 7.2 shows how players attempted to beat or avoid the defensive wall. The majority of free kicks were directed around (41 per cent) or over (36 per cent) the defensive wall. A surprisingly high proportion of shots (15 per cent) went through the defensive wall, perhaps highlighting some shortcomings in defensive organisation. The most surprising finding is that only 7 per cent of shots (11 from 152 attempts) were actually blocked by the defensive wall. Generally, the pattern of results is similar regardless of the distance or angle from goal.

Table 7.3 illustrates how the number of players in the defensive wall affected the execution of the free kick. Perhaps the main finding, although not an unexpected one, is that the likelihood of the ball being played around the wall (as opposed to over the wall) increases as the number of players in the wall decreases. If there are three or fewer players in the

Table 7.2 How players attempted to beat the defensive wall from direct shots at varying distances from goal in the 2002 World Cup

	18–23 yards	24–29 yards	30–35 yards	36+ yards	Total	%
Around	11	14	23	15	63	41
Over	3	26	21	4	54	36
Through	3	10	7	3	23	15
Blocked	3	3	1	4	7	11
Under	—	—	—	1	1	1
Total	20	53	52	27	152	100

Table 7.3 Influence of number of players in the wall on how free kicks were executed in the 2002 World Cup

No. of players	Around	Over	Through	Block	Under	Total	%
1	2	2	—	—	—	4	3
2	17	8	4	1	—	30	20
3	12	6	3	1	—	22	14
4	15	16	6	3	—	40	26
5	8	14	4	4	1	31	20
6	7	8	4	1	—	20	13
7	2	—	1	1	—	4	2
8	—	—	1	—	—	1	1
Total	63	54	23	11	1	152	100

wall, the ball is likely to travel around the wall, whereas if there are five or more players in the wall it is likely to be played over the wall. There may be implications here for trying to make the wall look as big as possible to distract the player taking the free kick, thereby pushing him/her to use the 'pass-and-shoot' strategy.

Attacking free kicks in wide areas

Table 7.4 indicates that in-swinging free kicks were slightly more successful than out-swinging free kicks from wide areas in the 2002 World Cup. The same trend was apparent in the 2000 European Championships. Although the effectiveness of different types of free kicks is determined by a range of factors, including the accuracy and quality of delivery and the movements and positioning of the attacking players, it appears that in-swinging free kicks towards the near-post region or out-swinging free kicks to the far post are most effective.

All goals scored from in-swinging free kicks were delivered into the central goal region between the penalty spot and the edge of the 6-yard box. However, a fairly high proportion of attempts on goal came from in-swinging free kicks delivered to the near-post region. There were very few attempts at goal from in-swinging free kicks delivered close to the goalkeeper or towards the far post and beyond. Moreover, in-swinging free kicks to the far post and beyond were more likely to lead to a counter-attack by the opposition. No counter-attacks were initiated from in-swinging free kicks directed to the near post. Implications are highlighted for the placement of defensive players to avoid counter-attacks at in-swinging free kicks.

The goals scored from out-swinging free kicks occurred when the ball was delivered to the mid-goal or far-post regions. Similarly, the vast majority of attempts at goal from out-swinging free kicks occurred when the ball was delivered beyond the penalty spot and towards the far-post region. In contrast, there was a far greater chance of being exposed to a counter-attack with an out-swinging free kick delivered to the near post compared with all the other categories.

Table 7.4 *Success rates of different types of free kicks from wide areas played directly into the penalty area in the 2002 World Cup*

	In-Swinging Near Post	In-Swinging Central	In-Swinging Far Post	In-Swinging Deep	Out-Swinging Near Post	Out-Swinging Central	Out-Swinging Far Post	Out-Swinging Deep
Total	22	43	19	12	13	60	32	22
Goals	—	2	—	—	—	1	2	—
Attempts on goal per free kick	1:7	1:9	1:10	1:12	1:13	1:11	1:5	1:22
Overall ratio			1:10				1:13	

Corner kicks

The success rates of different types of corner kicks in the World Cup 2002 are highlighted in Table 7.5. The majority of first- and second-phase goals come from a direct cross into the penalty area (18 out of 21 goals scored), although a short pass to change the angle of delivery followed by a cross into the penalty area had the highest success ratio (46 per cent).

The success rates of in-swinging and out-swinging corners are presented in Table 7.6. In-swinging corners are generally more successful in creating goals, although the chances of losing possession and being caught on the counter-attack are greater. These latter factors may be a small price to pay, given the improved chance of scoring. In-swinging corners appear to be more than three times as successful as out-swinging corners. A similar finding has been reported for domestic soccer, where in a recent survey more goals were scored from in-swinging (71 per cent) than out-swinging (29 per cent) corners.

The results of the analysis of corner kicks delivered into the penalty area were similar to that for free kicks from wide areas in both the 2000 European Championships and the 2002 World Cup. Specifically, in-swinging corners to the near-post and mid-goal region were most successful, although the chances of losing possession or being caught on the counter-attack are greater. Some success was also gained from out-swinging corners, particularly when directed between the penalty spot and the far post.

Table 7.5 *Success rates of different types of corner kicks in the 2002 World Cup*

	Attempts	Success (%) (proportion leading to attempt on goal)	First-phase goals	Second-phase goals	Total
Short	8	25	—	—	32
Short cross	29	46	3	—	63
Cross	189	34	10	8	555
Other	—		—	—	1
Total	226	35	13	8	651

Table 7.6 *Corners played directly into the penalty area in the 2002 World Cup*

	Total	Success (%) (proportion leading to goals)	Second-phase occurrence (%)	Loss of possession (%)	Counter attack (%)
In-swinging	244	6	32	33	7
Out-swinging	221	2	39	29	2

Corner-kick preparation time and attempts at goal

Figure 7.3 presents the proportion of attempts at goal from three different types of corner kicks as a function of preparation time in the 2002 World Cup. Short corner kicks are far more effective when the time from the corner kick being awarded to being executed is less than 20 seconds. Similarly, short corner kicks involving a pass and a direct cross into the box are also far more successful if taken quickly. In contrast, corner kicks played directly into the penalty area are more effective when the preparation time is greater than 20 seconds, thereby allowing teams to send defensive players into the attacking penalty area and to organise effectively for the expected ball delivery. Similar results were obtained for the 2000 European Championships.

Attacking throw-ins

A throw-in was the most common set play in the attacking third in the 2002 World Cup. On average, there were around 17 throw-ins awarded in the attacking third per game, the same number as were awarded in the 2000 European Championships. Slightly more goals (9 versus 3) were scored from throw-ins in the 2002 tournament compared with Euro 2000, with the majority of these goals coming from a short throw followed by a cross into the box (see Table 7.7). Surprisingly, almost as many goals (8) came from throw-ins in midfield compared with the attacking third. This latter finding may suggest that throw-ins merely provide a good opportunity to retain possession of the ball as opposed to creating a goal-scoring opportunity. The long throw was used infrequently and only one goal was scored in the whole tournament from this route. However, long throw-ins are a useful source of attempts at goal and/or for gaining other set plays, but the likelihood of losing possession and being faced with a counter-attack is higher than for short throws.

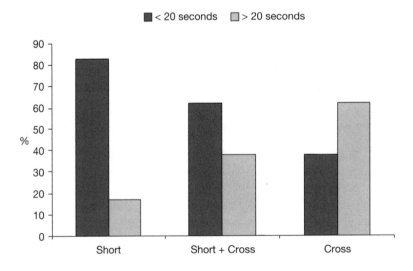

Figure 7.3 *Analysis of preparation time for corner kicks and attempts on goal (first phase only) in the 2002 World Cup*

Table 7.7 *Analysis of throw-ins from the attacking third in the 2002 World Cup*

	Short throw	Short throw + cross	Long throw	Total
Total	626	243	169	1038
First phase goals	2	5	0	7
Second phase goals	1	0	1	2
Success (%) (proportion leading to attempts on goal)	11	20	15	14

SOME OBSERVATIONS FROM OPEN PLAY: CREATING AND SCORING GOALS

Temporal analysis of goals scored

Figure 7.4 highlights the proportion of goals scored in each 15-minute period for the 1998 and 2002 World Cup tournaments respectively. The pattern of goal scoring is fairly consistent across the two tournaments, with more goals being scored as the game progresses, presumably as a result of the decrease in match tempo and the adoption of more adventurous attacking strategies. The number of goals scored in the second half of matches was 89, compared with 72 goals in the first half. The importance of players achieving high levels of fitness and concentration skills is highlighted, as well the effective use of substitutes and variations in attacking strategy by coaches.

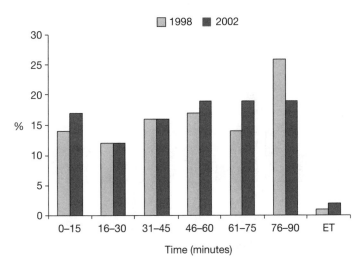

Figure 7.4 *Temporal analysis (in 15-minute intervals) of goals scored in the 1998 and 2002 World Cup finals*

The temporal distribution of goals scored is broken down into 3-minute intervals in Figure 7.5. As in the 1998 and 1994 World Cups, the majority of goals were scored early or late in each half, presumably because of fatigue or lack of concentration, or the adoption of a more attacking strategy as a result of having to 'chase the game' to try to avoid elimination from the tournament. In particular, the 'golden goal' rule may have encouraged teams to be particularly adventurous in the knockout stages of the tournament, with teams being more inclined to risk conceding in the later stages of 'normal' time rather than in extra time. More than half of the goals were scored in the opening and closing 6–9 minutes of each half (plus injury time).

In contrast, Figure 7.6 shows that in the 1997–1998 English Premiership, a higher than normal number of goals were scored in the 35- to 40-minute period.

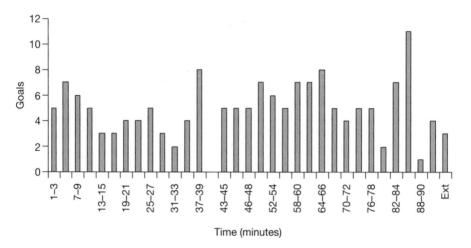

Figure 7.5 *Number of goals scored in 3-minute intervals in 2002 World Cup*

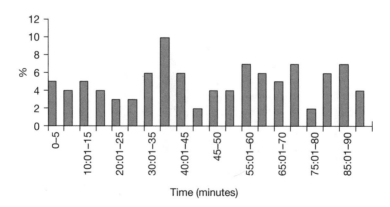

Figure 7.6 *Percentage of goals scored in 5-minute periods over the duration of a match in the 1997–1998 English Premiership*

Techniques used to score goals

The goal scorers employed a variety of different 'finishing' techniques in the 2002 World Cup, as highlighted in Table 7.8. The majority of goals during open play were scored with the laces part of the boot (27 per cent), followed closely by the inside of the foot and instep (approximately 22 per cent respectively). A reasonable proportion of goals were scored using the head (22 per cent), slightly up from the 1998 World Cup (18 per cent), with the majority of these coming from set plays. A very small percentage of goals were scored with the outside of the foot (3 per cent). Nearly all penalties were struck with the instep or inside of the foot, with only one penalty been executed using the laces part of the boot. This latter finding suggests an emphasis on placement rather than power by successful penalty takers. One significant difference between domestic and international soccer is that more goals are scored with the head in the English professional leagues.

Table 7.9 shows the number of touches used by the goal scorer prior to and including the finishing touch during open and set plays. The majority of goals were scored using a

Table 7.8 Techniques used to score goals in 2002 World Cup

	Open play	Penalties	Set play	Second-phase play	Total	Percentage
Inside	18	7	—	10	35	22
Outside	3	—	2	—	5	3
Instep	17	5	7	5	34	21
Laces	25	1	5	12	43	27
Head	14	—	19	3	36	22
Toe	4	—	—	—	4	2
Trunk	1	—	—	—	1	1
Shoulder	—	—	—	1	1	1
Shin	1	—	—	1	2	1
Total	83	13	33	32	161	100

Table 7.9 Number of touches used to score a goal in the 2002 World Cup

No. of touches	Open play	Set play	Second-phase play	Total	Percentage
1	57	45	24	126	78
2	14	—	5	19	12
3	5	—	2	7	4
4	3	1	—	4	2
5	2	—	—	2	1
6	—	—	—	0	0
7	1	—	—	1	1
8	—	—	1	1	1
9	1	—	—	1	1
Total	83	46	32	161	100

one-touch finish, with very few goals (around 10 per cent) being scored when players took more than two touches on the ball. Implications for developing effective shooting drills are highlighted. No comparable data are available for domestic soccer.

Areas from where goals were scored

The data presented in Table 7.10 show that in the 2002 World Cup the majority of goals were scored from inside the penalty area, specifically the area between the edge of the 6-yard box and the penalty spot (37 per cent of goals). In the 2002 World Cup, slightly more goals were scored from shots outside the box (24 goals) compared with 1998 (17 goals), with the figure for 2002 being comparable to that for the 1994 World Cup Finals (20 goals). No comparable data are available for domestic soccer.

Table 7.10 *Distance of the final strike from goal in the 2002 World Cup (excluding penalty kicks)*

0–6 yards	7–12 yards	12–18 yards	19–24 yards	24–30 yards	30+ yards
29%	37%	18%	9%	6%	1%

Number of passes and time in possession prior to goals scored from open play

The number of passes prior to a goal being scored in the 1998 and 2002 World Cup tournaments is provided in Figure 7.7. The majority of goals were scored following sequences of play involving between 1 and 4 passes. A reasonable proportion of goals were scored from sequences of play involving five or more passes in the 2002 tournament (34 per cent), a figure slightly up on the 1998 World Cup (26 per cent). Of particular note is that during the 2002 tournament a total of 5 goals (6 per cent) were scored following sequences of play involving more than 11 passes.

The pattern for English domestic soccer is somewhat similar to that highlighted in Figure 7.7. However, higher proportions of goals are scored from shorter passing sequences in the Premier League and fewer from long passing sequences. The majority of goals scored from open play in the Premiership involve build-ups with zero passes (e.g. a 'snap shot' following a clearance or rebound) or one pass. In the 1998 World Cup, 3-pass moves provided the highest frequency of goals from open play, indicating the more possession-oriented style of play favoured by international teams. These differences are highlighted in Figure 7.8.

The time in possession prior to a goal being scored in the 2002 World Cup is highlighted in Table 7.11. The majority (53 per cent) of goals were scored after periods of possession lasting between 6 and 15 seconds; a smaller yet significant proportion of goals were scored after possession lasting 0 to 5 seconds and 21 to 25 seconds. The findings are generally similar to those reported for the 1998 World Cup, although one notable difference is the fact that a higher proportion of goals were scored after periods of possession lasting more than 21 seconds in 2002 (24 per cent) compared with 1998 (16 per cent).

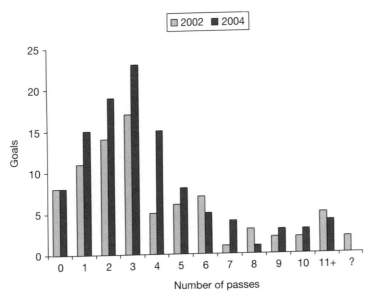

Figure 7.7 *Number of passes prior to a goal being scored in open play in the 1998 and 2002 World Cups*

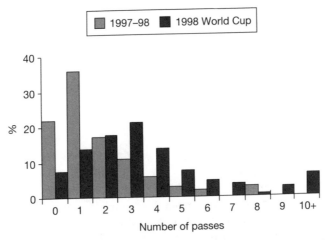

Figure 7.8 *Number of passes prior to a goal being scored from open play in the 1997–98 English Premiership and the 1998 World Cup*

Tables 7.12 and 7.13 highlight the periods of time for which teams maintained possession of the ball prior to a goal being scored. Most goals in the Premiership were scored following possession of 2 seconds or less. Over 55 per cent of all goals scored in the Premiership resulted from a build-up of less than 5 seconds. This is in contrast to the 1998 and 2002 World Cups, where only 20 per cent and 16 per cent respectively of goals scored during open play came from build-ups lasting 0–5 seconds. Teams in the World

Table 7.11 *Time in possession prior to a goal in open play in the 2002 World Cup*

Time (seconds)	Total	Percentage
0–5	13	16
6–10	25	30
11–15	19	23
16–20	3	4
21–25	9	11
26–30	4	5
31–35	2	2
36–40	4	5
41–45	0	0
46–50	0	0
51–55	0	0
56–60	0	0
60+	1	1
Unknown	3	3
Total	83	100

N.B. Three goals could not be coded, because of the nature of the television coverage.

Table 7.12 *Time in possession prior to a goal in open play in the 1997–1998 Premiership*

Time (seconds)	Percentage of goals
0–2	33
3–5	23
6–8	14
9–11	11
12+	19

Cup scored more than 50 per cent of goals from build-ups lasting 12 seconds or more, compared to just 19 per cent for the Premiership. These findings suggest that international teams are more likely to score goals following a longer period of possession and imply that in the Premiership teams tend to employ a more 'direct' attacking strategy. In

Table 7.13 *Time in possession prior to a goal in open play in the 1997–1998 Premiership and 1998 World Cup*

Time (seconds)	1997–1998 Premiership (%)	1998 World Cup (%)
0–5	56	19
6–11	26	26
12+	18	55

HANDBOOK OF SOCCER MATCH ANALYSIS

contrast, at the 1999 Women's World Cup very few attempts on goal or goals came from passing sequences lasting longer than 12 seconds, more closely mirroring findings from the Premier League than from the 1998 and 2002 men's World Cups.

In summary, although most goals are scored following sequences of play lasting between 6 and 10 seconds and involving fewer than 3 passes, successful teams (e.g. France 1998 and 2000, Manchester United 1999, Brazil 2002) are also able to create more goals than the opposition following longer passing sequences. The key factor may be having players who are technically proficient such that opportunities can be taken when need be or that possession can be maintained until a suitable attacking opportunity arises.

The general trends are that successful teams, whether in domestic or international soccer, have the ability to vary their style of play and are able to score a higher proportion of goals than unsuccessful teams following short (e.g. moves of 3 passes or fewer and less than 10 seconds in possession) and long (e.g. more than 8 passes and 25 seconds in possession) periods of possession.

Key events preceding goals scored in open play

The major 'goal assists' during the 2002 World Cup tournament are highlighted in Table 7.14. The majority of goals were preceded by either a pass or a cross. The proportion of goals scored following a pass was significantly lower in 2002 than in the 1998 World Cup, where 47 per cent of goals were scored following a pass assist. Similarly, the proportion of goals following a turn or dribble was slightly lower in 2002 (14 per cent) than in 1998 (20 per cent). In contrast, the proportion of goals scored from crosses was much higher in 2002 (29 per cent) than in 1998 (18 per cent).

In the past, crosses were mainly played into the penalty areas from wide areas between the penalty area and the touchline or from 'cut-backs' from the goal line. As highlighted in Figure 7.9, cross assists now tend to originate from all areas of the field. It appears that players are able to create sufficient spin and swerve on the ball to deliver effective crosses even from central areas of the field.

Table 7.14 *Key event preceding goals scored in open play in the 2002 World Cup*

Key event preceding goal	Total number	Percentage
Pass	24	29
Cross	24	29
Tackle/intercept	10	12
GK rebound	6	7
Cut-back	2	2
Individual play (dribble etc.)	12	14
Clearance	3	4
Headed pass	2	2
Total	83	100

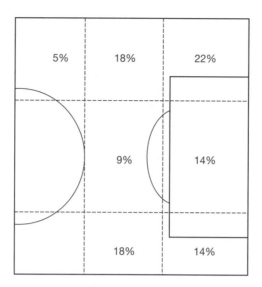

Figure 7.9 *Areas from where crosses (including cut-backs) leading to goals were played in the 2002 World Cup*

In English domestic soccer, most goals come from pass assists. One important difference is that more goals are scored from crosses (i.e., headers and volleys) in the Premier League than in international soccer, as illustrated by data from an analysis of Manchester United in 1999 and previous published literature. Regardless of the fact that more goals are scored from crosses in domestic compared with international soccer, the importance of creativity in central attacking areas has increased in recent years even in the domestic game. Successful teams are able to penetrate the opposition's defence more effectively than less successful teams with a telling pass from a central area just outside the penalty box (see Figure 7.10). For example, in the 1998 World Cup successful teams played an average of 25 passes per match from central areas, with 70 per cent of these passes being in a forward direction compared to 15 passes per game for less successful teams, with only 63 per cent of these being forward. Also, in the 1998 World Cup and 2000 European Championships, France scored more than half its goals from a pass assist initiated in this area of the field, whereas in the 2002 World Cup this area was again the most important area for pass assists.

In the English Premiership, teams have possession of the ball in the area highlighted in Figure 7.10 an average of 30 times per match, with 26 per cent of these possessions leading to an attempt on goal. Dribbling with the ball, turning with the ball and short forward diagonal passes were the most successful actions leading to attempts on goal in this area of the field. Perhaps surprisingly, wall passes (one-twos) were relatively ineffective in creating chances, possibly as a result of defensive units playing slightly deeper than might have been the case in the past. Implications for coaching practice are evident.

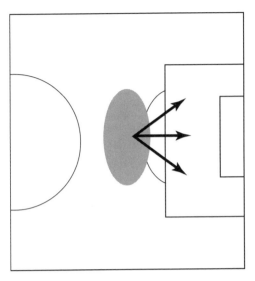

Figure 7.10 *The highlighted area is an important area for creative play in the attacking third*

Regained possession resulting in goals scored from open play

The area of the field where possession was regained prior to a goal being scored in open play during the 2002 World Cup is shown in Table 7.15. Regained possession was defined as the moment the scoring team secured possession following, for example, a tackle, interception or set play. The proportion of goals scored after regaining possession in the attacking third was fairly low (20 per cent) when compared with the midfield (51 per cent) and defensive (29 per cent) thirds. Altogether, 64 per cent of goals were scored after possession had been regained in the defensive half and almost 11 per cent of goals were scored after possession had been regained inside the defensive penalty area. The ability to score goals when possession is regained in defensive positions would appear crucial to success in international soccer. This latter finding may highlight the important role played by the goalkeeper in initiating offensive play through effective distribution of the ball. It may also indicate that teams hold a fairly deep defensive line (i.e. just outside the defensive penalty area) at this level of soccer.

Table 7.15 *Total number and proportion of goals scored from open play across defending, midfield and attacking thirds in the 2002 World Cup*

	Total number	Percentage
Defending	24	29
Midfield	42	51
Attacking	17	20
Totals	83	100

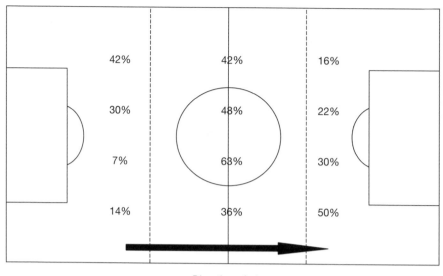

Direction of play

Figure 7.11 *Percentage of regained possession in different parts of the field resulting in a goal from open play for (in order of presentation, (top to bottom) Brazil (2002 World Cup), teams in the 1998 World Cup, Manchester United (1999) and teams in the Premier League (1997–1998)*

Figure 7.11 presents comparative data on areas of regained possession leading to a goal for teams in the 1998 World Cup, Brazil (World Cup 2002), Manchester United (1999) and the Premier League (1997–1998). It appears that in domestic soccer, teams may play more of a pressing game than in international soccer, with more goals being scored after possession has been regained in midfield (36 per cent) and attacking areas (50 per cent) rather than in the defensive third (14 per cent). The findings for the Premier League are comparable to those for the 1999 Women's World Cup, where the percentage of goals scored after regaining possession in the defensive, midfield and attacking thirds were 28 per cent, 19 per cent and 53 per cent respectively.

A similar trend is observed for areas of regained possession resulting in attempts on goal (rather than goals). In international soccer, more attempts on goal arise following regained possession in midfield, whereas in domestic soccer more attempts arise when the ball is regained in the attacking third. There are two important points to highlight:

■ The quality of build-up play and the chance of scoring may be higher when the ball is regained further away from goal. Play may be more structured and deliberate. Alternatively, this finding may highlight the importance of fast counter-attacking play, given that most goals are scored after periods of possession lasting less than 15 seconds and involving fewer than four passes.

■ In English domestic soccer, teams generally play further up the field than international teams, perhaps holding a defensive line nearer the half-way line and generally playing more of a pressing game to regain possession of the ball in the opposition's defensive third.

Scoring efficiency/strike rate

Successful teams have a higher proportion of goals scored relative to attempts on goal, highlighting the importance of having quality players who can take full advantage of goal-scoring opportunities. In the 2002 World Cup, Brazil had a goal scored to attempt on goal ratio of 1:5 from open play and 1:7 from set plays. Similarly, in the 1998 World Cup and Euro 2000, France's ratios were 1:7 from open play and 1:6 from set play, whereas during its treble-winning season in 1999, Manchester United's corresponding ratios were 1:9 and 1:6 respectively. As highlighted in Table 7.16, the number of goals scored relative to attempts on goal for less successful teams is much lower, with on average 18 attempts on goal being needed before a goal is scored.

CONSECUTIVE FORWARD MOVEMENT

Successful teams in domestic and international soccer are more likely to adopt patterns of play that involve running, dribbling and passing the ball continuously in a forward direction. For example, a forward pass followed by a forward run with the ball and another forward pass would be a move involving three consecutive forward movements of the ball. The mean frequencies of moves involving consecutive forward movements of varying lengths for successful and unsuccessful teams in the 1998 and 2002 World Cups are highlighted in Table 7.17.

The ability to move the ball forward in a consecutive manner suggests that successful teams are able to penetrate the opposition's defensive lines better than less successful teams. A recent analysis of Brazil's performances in the 2002 World Cup also showed that nearly every player was more inclined to play the ball forward than was his counterpart on the opposition team. The key point perhaps is that successful teams have players in all areas of the field who are more comfortable on the ball and are able to run, dribble or pass the ball more effectively than those playing for less successful teams. The importance of having players who are comfortable on the ball and with good technical ability is thus illustrated.

Table 7.16 *Ratios of goal to attempts on goal for successful teams and their opponents in recent tournaments*

Successful teams	Open play	Set play
France – World Cup 1998/Euro 2000	1:7	1:6
Brazil – World Cup 2002	1:5	1:7
Manchester United – 1999	1:9	1:6
Average Ratio	1:7	
France's opponents – World Cup 1998/Euro 2000	1:28	1:5
Brazil's opponents – World Cup 2002	1:15	1:36
Manchester United's opponents 1999	1:18	1:8
Average ratio	1:18	

Table 7.17 *Average number of consecutive forward movements of the ball per match for successful and unsuccessful teams in the 1998 and 2002 World Cups*

Number of consecutive forward ball movements	Successful	Unsuccessful
2	42.3	32.5
3	32.1	22.5
4	17.7	11.6
5	8.1	5.5
6	4.5	2.4
7	2.5	1.5
8	1.2	0.6
9	0.8	0.2
10+	0.3	0.2
Total	109.5	77.0

Keeping the ball

The ability to maintain possession of the ball enables teams to control the structure and tempo of the game and, not surprisingly, successful teams enjoy longer passing sequences on average than less successful teams. The majority of passing sequences for successful and less successful teams involve between 1 and 5 passes. However, in the 2002 World Cup less successful teams had a higher proportion of sequences involving 1 to 5 passes than successful teams (92 per cent versus 77 per cent), whereas, in contrast, successful teams had a higher proportion of moves involving between 6 and 10 passes than less successful teams (23 versus 8 per cent).

Similarly, in an analysis of Premier League matches in 1996–1997, teams that maintained possession of the ball more than the opposition were far less likely to lose the match, particularly if the difference in possession rates between teams was greater than 8 per cent. Teams that had less possession during a game ended up winning the match on 21 per cent of occasions, whereas teams that had more possession ended up winning the match almost 50 per cent of the time.

Tempo of matches

The data presented in Table 7.18 suggest that the tempo/speed of domestic soccer is higher than in international soccer, as determined by a frequency count of key match actions from the 1998 World Cup and Premier League. For example, there are more dribbles with the ball, crosses, headers and passes in English domestic compared with international soccer. There are also more passes played in the air as opposed to along the ground in domestic compared with international soccer. These data testify to the frantic pace of the Premier League.

Table 7.18 *Frequency of key match actions per game*

Match actions	1998 World Cup	1998 Premier League
Runs with ball	87	70
Dribble with ball	77	142
Crosses	16	41
Headers	49	140
Passes	335	541
Lofted passes	70	114

SUMMARY

The aim of this chapter was to review recent match analysis literature in an attempt to highlight potentially important implications for coaches. The information presented was not meant to be overly prescriptive, but rather was intended to extend the coach's professional knowledge in this area and to try to differentiate between subjective opinion and objective data. The manner in which the data are interpreted and applied rests with the coach, illustrating the important balance between craft and professional knowledge in successful coaching. It is acknowledged that not all the findings are likely to be surprising to the experienced coach, but equally it is important for all coaches to distinguish where possible between subjective opinion and objective data. The main take-home messages for coaches are the following:

1   Set plays occur less frequently in international compared with the domestic soccer game. Set plays are awarded less frequently than in previous years, although a higher proportion of goals are now scored from set plays, with free kicks, followed by corners, being the most productive.
2   Most free kicks in the attacking third are awarded after a player has been fouled when running at a defender with the ball.
3   The most successful strategy at direct free kicks in the attacking third is the direct shot, with the 'pass-and-shoot' strategy being relatively unsuccessful.
4   In-swinging free kicks are generally more successful than out-swinging free kicks from wide areas. In-swinging kicks are most successful when directed to the near-post or mid-goal region, whereas out-swinging kicks to the mid-goal or far-post region are also important. An interesting point is that in-swinging free kicks to the near post are also more easily intercepted than those to other parts of the penalty area (i.e. there is difficulty in clearing the first defender), so there may be implications for making this player look as big as possible so that free kicks are 'overhit'. These conclusions apply almost equally well to corner kicks played directly into the penalty area.
5   Short corners (i.e., a pass followed by a cross) can be effective if taken quickly. There is no urgency when the corner is to be played directly into the box.

6   Throw-ins provide an excellent opportunity to maintain ball possession, whereas a throw followed by a cross into the box can provide a goal-scoring opportunity. Long throws are used infrequently in international matches and relatively few goals are scored, although they can provide a good source of attempts at goal and result in other set plays.

7   Most goals in international soccer are scored early or late in each half, whereas in the Premier League more goals are scored mid-way through the first half than at other times.

8   In English domestic soccer, most goals are scored from moves lasting 0–5 seconds and involving 2 passes or fewer, whereas in international soccer most goals involve 3–5 passes and the moves leading to them last 6–10 seconds. Also, in international soccer more goals are scored from moves involving more than 10 passes and lasting longer than 15 seconds compared with domestic soccer.

9   A pass is the key assist in domestic and international soccer, although more than twice as many goals are scored from across in domestic soccer as compared with international soccer.

10   When goals are scored in domestic soccer, the ball is typically regained in the attacking third, whereas in international soccer most goals are scored following the regaining of possession in the midfield and defensive thirds.

11   Successful teams have a higher success rate in converting chances into goals than do less successful teams, particularly in international soccer.

12   The tempo may well be higher in domestic soccer compared with international soccer as determined by a frequency count of key actions per match.

CHAPTER EIGHT

▼ FROM TECHNICAL AND TACTICAL PERFORMANCE ANALYSIS TO TRAINING DRILLS

INTRODUCTION

In this chapter we provide practical examples and advice on how to apply the results effectively from tactical and technical match analysis to soccer training programmes. Different scenarios are described using the match analysis process to help optimise training with the ultimate aim of improving playing performance. Detailed information is also provided on what can be analysed from a tactical and technical point of view, as well as ideas on using match analysis and feedback during training sessions.

STRATEGY, PLAYING SYSTEMS, TACTICS AND TECHNIQUE

Soccer is a team sport involving strategic, tactical and technical dimensions which give rise to different forms of coaching questions and knowledge. It is therefore important to define and understand these dimensions, since when analysed they are the difference between winning and losing.

- Match strategy may be defined as a system or method of team operation based upon the combined capabilities of players.
- Playing systems involve the creation of a framework, through the organisation and deployment of players, which the team uses to try to implement match strategy.
- Tactics are the individual and collective ways used by a team to best employ player skills in order to make the overall strategy work by either scoring or preventing goals.

1   Individual tactics are based on how the individual player reacts in certain match situations and are often used when in contact with an opposing player (e.g. making space or marking).
2   Group tactics are based on cooperation between several members or units of the same team who work together to achieve their goal (e.g. the offside trap or space coverage).
3   Team tactics are the offensive and defensive methods adopted by the team as a whole to counter the opposition's game plan (e.g. playing for time, or setting up counter-attacks).

■   Skill is the ability to apply the appropriate technique in a range of situations so as to result in stable and consistent performance. Technique is the way in which movements or actions, such as controlling the ball, are performed. Technique is only one part of soccer skill, as the player primarily relies on his/her skill to select and correctly employ the required technique on demand as a result of the information provided by the game situation. A player with great shooting technique may not have either the physical or the mental skills needed to get into a decent shooting position in the first place. Likewise, a fast player may not have the technical skill required to run at pace with the ball.

These dimensions of match play allow us to define the basic principles of the game. These principles are the foundations for developing and implementing strategies, playing systems and tactics, and can give rise to the analysis and evaluation of match performance. There are three principal phases to the game: attacking play to create scoring chances and goals; defensive play to prevent scoring chances and goals; and midfield play, which involves reorganisation when building up attacking play or defending against the opposition's build-up. In other words, ball possession determines everything in soccer. In order to put these game principles into practice successfully, the following individual and team aspects of play are essential:

■   high-quality pitch and zone coverage in terms of width and length when defending and attacking;
■   high-quality pitch organisation, movement and support based on positional play and distance between players and units;
■   high-quality attacking skills relying on space creation, penetration, width, mobility, improvisation, and capacity to change the tempo, switch play and switch from defence to attack;
■   high-quality defending skills relying on support, reducing space, depth, delay, concentration, balance, control and the ability to regain possession.

Success in soccer is dependent on all the above principles, and it is only by analysing and evaluating these particular factors that a complete picture and understanding of match performance can be established.

WHAT TECHNICAL AND TACTICAL ASPECTS CAN BE ANALYSED?

The general principles of the game are listed in the previous section, and various examples of what can be analysed in performance from a tactical and technical point of view are provided in Chapter 5. It is always useful to look in even greater detail at these game principles in order to suggest ways in which they can be qualitatively and quantitatively analysed. These suggestions may generate different coaching ideas on ways of detecting strengths and weaknesses in strategies, playing systems, tactics and techniques. Furthermore, through the evaluation of the information provided by match analysis, different training sessions can be designed and employed. Tables 8.1–8.3 provide a qualitative list (by no means exhaustive) of ideas on the analysis of various match factors as well as suggestions on how these can be looked at quantitatively from an individual, unit and team point of view.

COACHING TACTICS AND TECHNIQUE USING MATCH ANALYSIS AND FEEDBACK

The strategy used to achieve an overall aim in soccer relies on the successful application of both individual and team tactics and techniques. As the match analysis process tends to concentrate on providing information about tactical (e.g. effectiveness of playing style) and technical (e.g. passing success rates) performance, the process is particularly relevant in understanding performance and suggesting areas for improvement.

Coaches must carefully plan and organise daily training with the single aim of providing optimal preparation for competition. The process of successfully devising practice situations which can then be transferred into competitive performance is one of the key roles of any coach. Relevant and effective training sessions can be devised and carried out on the basis of actual match performance information (whether statistical or descriptive or both) provided from manual or computerised match analysis.

Before planning, deciding on and undertaking training sessions based on the results gleaned from match analysis, the coach must have fully evaluated and understood the findings. Only then can the resulting training sessions be chosen and put into practice. Feedback on areas which need to be worked on must have been given previously to players during individual and/or team talks. Similarly, future sessions and drills based on this information must also have been discussed (see Chapter 5 for advice on team talks). A practical model of the different steps of the match analysis process is presented in Figure 8.1. In order to increase coaching effectiveness, the players need to know why and how they will practise certain tactical and technical drills. If a team has struggled in one particular area of match play such as set plays, then the coach needs to have highlighted where the players went wrong before suggesting ways of improving performance through the conception and practising of various drills.

The general aim of tactical and technical training is to improve the decision-making and application of game actions using different and realistic playing situations. Feedback from video and match simulations may also be used to aid player understanding and learning of various tactical issues, although it is of course on the pitch where players experience

Table 8.1 *General team analysis* (qualitative *and quantitative*)

Playing system	4–4–2, 4–3–3, 4–5–1, 3–5–2. Flexible or rigid, changes in system according to ball possession
	Defensive and offensive zone maps of on- and off-the-ball possession, average positions to define team system
Team shape	Player positions and zone coverage
	Defensive and offensive zone maps containing 'on-' and 'off-the-ball' possession, average positions to define team shape
Playing style	Direct, slow build-up, counter-attacking
	Speed of attacks, average number of actions in attacks, time in possession
Defensive play	Offside trap, zone or man marking, deep or push up, do all the players contribute?
	Number of offside decisions won, zone coverage maps, number of duels won in different zones, interceptions, free kicks conceded
Attacking play	How are chances created, using which route and who is involved, who passes to whom, are attacks alternated (fast or slow play)?
	Number of goals, shots, crosses, corners and free kicks won, entrées into final third, last action type before shot, possession on wings or in central areas, zone coverage maps of balls played, passing patterns between individuals
Defensive set plays	Organisation, positioning, number of players defending, do they attack the ball, goalkeeping contribution
	Number of goals and shots conceded, heading clearance success rates, goalkeeper catches and punches
Attacking set plays	Players involved in taking and receiving, quickly taken, attacking numbers, inswinging or outswinging ball delivery, floated, near or far post, short corners, quickly taken moves, short throw-ins, improvisation, shooting quality
	Number of shots or goals scored, chances created, number of balls into near/far post, short corners, average time before set piece is played

and learn the most. Varied and step-by-step practice taking into account the player's individual abilities must be combined with correct coaching methods (e.g. verbal explanations and demonstrations with and without the ball, freezing play) to enhance the learning process. Training sessions should be based on the exact requirements of the game from both an individual and a team point of view. It is also advisable to evaluate tactical and technical performance in training further according to the aim of the exercise.

Table 8.2 *Analysis of team units* (qualitative *and quantitative*)

Team unit defensive analysis

Defensive unit   Zonal or player marking, cooperation with goalkeeper/midfield, quality of challenges, space reduction, depth, width, control

Number of duels attempted and won or lost, zone coverage maps of defending positions, number and position of free kicks and penalties conceded, cautions, offside decisions won

Midfield unit   Zonal or player marking, tracking back, cooperation with attack/defence, challenging for the ball, reducing space

Number of duels attempted and won or lost, balls won back in opposition half, zone coverage maps of defending positions, number and position of free kicks conceded

Attacking unit   Who contributes to defensive play and disrupts build-up?

Number of duels attempted, won or lost, balls won back in opposition half, zone coverage maps of defending positions

Team unit attacking analysis

Defensive unit   Do defenders get forward, quality of link-up play with midfield and attack, who is dangerous in the air?

Zone coverage maps of balls played, passing success rates between defence and midfield/attack, number of attacking duels won and shots

Midfield unit   Do midfielders get forward, quality of link-up play with attack, runs from deep, creating space, shooting ability, capacity to turn defence into attack and create chances?

Zone coverage maps of balls played, passing success rates between midfield and defence/attack, number of assists (last action before a goal), key passes (last action before a non-scoring shot), shooting effectiveness, number of duels won and lost

Attacking unit   Quality of link-up play with midfield, off the ball runs, creating space, shooting ability, capacity to win free kicks, duels and to create chances, dribbles, shots to goals ratio

Passing success rates between defence and midfield, number of assists, key passes, shots on target, crosses, duels won and lost, successful dribbles, offside decisions against, free kicks won

Table 8.3 *Individual player analysis* (qualitative *and quantitative)*

Individual defensive analysis

Goalkeeper   Positioning behind defence, ability to deal with shots, crosses, corners, one on ones, tends to punch, catch, quality of clearances

Number of goals conceded, saves, balls punched and caught, balls dropped, number of mistakes

Defenders   Aerial strength, tackling ability, reading the game, pressing

Number of interceptions, tackles, headers, zone coverage maps of defending positions, number and position of free kicks conceded

Midfielders   Does the player track back, is there an anchorman who is strong defensively, nuisance players, lacks self-control or discipline?

Number of duels attempted and won or lost, interceptions, zone coverage maps of defending positions, number and position of free kicks conceded, cautions

Attackers   Who tracks back, challenges and disrupts play?

Number of duels attempted, won or lost, zone coverage maps of defending positions

Individual attacking analysis

Goalkeeper   Throws, kicking, which foot, range, accuracy, direction, players aimed for

Number and percentage success rate of passes

Defenders   Who is comfortable on the ball and brings the ball out of defence, overlapping fullbacks, dangerous in the opponents' box, provides dangerous passes, long or short distribution?

Number and percentage success rate of passes, shots and headers in the opponents' box, zone coverage maps to see who gets forward or stays back

Midfielders   Main playmakers, who runs with the ball, who plays safe or offensively, who touches the ball the most, provides the most goal assists, shoots, crosses, off-the-ball runs from deep, dribbling?

Number and success in passing, goal assists, shots on target, dribbles, crosses, duels, goals, zone coverage maps to see who gets forward or stays back

Attackers   Main target player, who is strong on the ball, in the air, shields the ball, shooting and crossing ability, makes space, gets wide, runs behind the defence, strong in one-on-one situations, dribbling, gets on the end of crosses, good first touch?

Number and success in passing, goal assists, shots on target, dribbles, crosses, duels, goals, zone coverage maps to see who stays central or wide

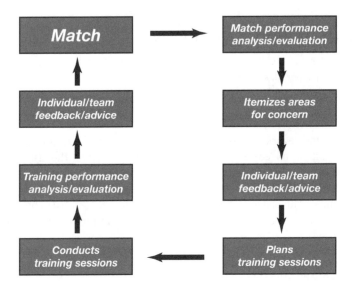

Figure 8.1 *The different steps of the match analysis process*

Finding the right balance between instructions, practical demonstrations and feedback on actual training performance is important and often depends on the knowledge and experience of the coach. Constructive, positive, accurate and relevant feedback on performance must be given whenever possible. Feedback should always relate to the players' skill level. The quantity and frequency of feedback are also important. Too much feedback can hinder progress and prevent players from improving their own skills, owing to their becoming over-dependent on their coach's advice. Players must efficiently develop their own error detection and correction skills in order to evaluate their personal performance, especially when the coach is not present. For example, a set-play specialist may have to try several techniques for striking free kicks at goal before settling on one preferred technique. A more 'hands-off' approach to instruction may help develop more adaptable players.

PRACTICAL APPLICATION

These practical examples of tactical and technical match analysis demonstrate all the different phases of the match analysis process. A coach can initially analyse performance, then evaluate the results. Examples of performance feedback are then given to players. The results and feedback are then applied in various training drills. For each individual scenario the performance situation and the methods used to observe and analyse the situation are described. Examples of the results obtained are then evaluated. Feedback is given to the players and selected examples of relevant training drills provided. Finally, drill organisation, description, variations and advice on how to analyse and evaluate the performance during practice are given.

CROSSING ANALYSIS SCENARIO

This scenario provides a practical example of the match analysis process used to examine crossing performance.

Situation

In the post-match review the coach feels that the team had a lot of possession but lacked width and produced very few crosses. Additionally, over the last few matches the centre-forwards seem to be struggling to get on the end of any crosses played into the penalty box. The team plays a 4–4–2 system and the team strategy is to encourage and create space to allow the fullbacks to get forward. The team is not conceding goals, but seems to be over-relying on its two forward players to create scoring chances.

Observation and analysis methods

The club is using the very latest in player tracking technology to analyse all aspects of performance. The coach asks the club's match analyst to provide detailed statistics on ball possession, crosses and chances created and zone coverage. These statistics will be used by the coach to back up the next team-talk presentation. The match analyst also works on producing an edited video presentation of attacking actions linked to a two-dimensional match reconstruction to complement the statistics.

Evaluation

Having compiled the information, the match analysis provides the coach with a report which is then evaluated. The report shows the following:

- The team had 59 per cent ball possession.
- Only 5 clear scoring chances were created, with two shots on goal.
- Only 2 crosses were made by the fullbacks, with neither leading to a scoring chance.
- Only 7 ball touches were made by the fullbacks in deep attacking positions on the wing.
- On- and off-the-ball zone coverage maps show that the fullbacks did not get forward and stayed relatively deep.
- Ninety per cent of attacking match actions took place in central areas.
- A further analysis over the last five matches shows that only 2 crosses out of 10 found an attacking player in the penalty area.

Feedback

The coach gets the team together to discuss the lack of penetration in wing areas. The players are presented with the statistical performance and the edited video and match reconstruction. The coach also mentions that around a third of goals come from crosses in top-flight soccer and that this is the level the team should be aiming towards. Using a list of selected attacks, the players visualise the action and are 'walked' through instances where the fullbacks could and should have got forward. The match reconstruction allows the coach to highlight clearly the fullback's positions in relation to the ball, especially as this information is not always available on the video. The coach tries to make the problem a team issue and not to alienate these particular players. Finally, the session finishes with the two instances of good performance where the fullbacks managed to get a cross in, and the players are asked to comment on the differences in performance.

The coach then moves on to the problem of the two strikers getting on the end of the crosses. The strikers feel that they are spending too much time out wide trying to create width for the team and therefore are not getting into the penalty area. The coach assures the strikers that the fullbacks will contribute more to the attack and that they should concentrate on the timing of their runs into the box. Satisfied that the players have understood where they are going wrong, the coach then sets the fullbacks a realistic target of three crosses each per match and challenges the forwards to get on the end of at least two of these crosses.

Training

At the end of the session, the coach presents the week's training content and how it will be planned. The main focus of the week will be to practise attacking drills based on getting fullbacks to overlap and cross in deep attacking positions and improving the movement in the penalty area of the two centre-forwards to get on the end of crosses.

Organisation

Pitch of around three-quarters length, 8 attackers versus 4 defenders + goalkeeper. Attacking team contains 4 defenders, 2 midfielders and 2 attackers.

Description

The game starts with defender no. 4 (Dark circle, Figure 8.2)m who plays the ball forward to midfield no. 7, who turns and plays it into no. 9 dropping off the defender. No. 9 plays the ball with one touch back to midfield no. 8 in support, who plays a one-touch pass out wide to the fullback, who has moved forward.

Variations/progressions

- Add more defending midfield players.
- Vary pitch size, add zones to limit player movements.
- Vary passes (e.g. to feet, in the air . . .) and encourage passes to every player.
- Transition into a small-sided game and eventually into 11 versus 11.

Further analysis and evaluation

The coach should be analysing the build-up in the middle to create space out wide for the fullback. The numerical attacking superiority should allow the predetermined moves to be carried out. Midfielders must concentrate on creating space and the fullbacks must work on the timing of their runs in relation to the ball and defenders' positions. Each attack should end in a shot at goal, therefore good movement off-the-ball and crossing are vital.

Performance can be evaluated by giving points for the number of shooting chances

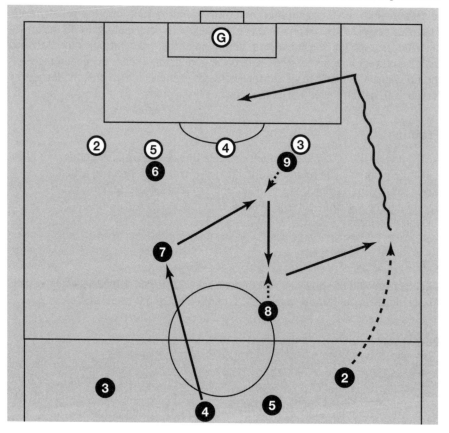

Figure 8.2 *A training drill to create width through overlapping fullbacks*

and goals created compared to the number of times the defence won back possession or cleared the danger.

Organisation

- Two servers, 2 crossing players and 2 players in the middle to get on the end of the cross.
- Large supply of balls.

Description

The game starts on the left wing (Figure 8.3). The first server plays the fullback in, who crosses first time into the penalty area. The crosses must be high quality (e.g. of the right pace and height).

No. 9 must time the run to get in a shot or header on goal.

Once the action has finished, the second server plays the ball to no. 2, who crosses for no. 8.

The players in the middle can switch sides after 5 crosses.

Description/progressions

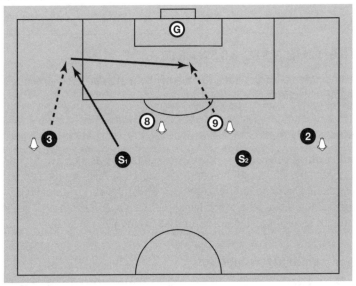

Figure 8.3 *Example of a training drill to work on the timing of attacking runs to get on the end of crosses*

The players can initially be 'walked' through the drill to help improve run timing and angle in order to increase their chances of getting on the end of the cross and to get the best possible contact on the ball.

- Add defenders to disrupt play.
- Vary crosses (to feet, in the air, near the post . . .).
- Have both players moving in for the same cross.
- Add midfield players and further defenders for the build-up phase.
- Progress to a conditioned small-sided game and eventually into 11 versus 11.

Further analysis and evaluation

The coach is concentrating on the runs made by the forwards and is looking at three major factors: the angle and timing of the run and the contact made with the ball. When a defender is introduced, the coach should be looking at the determination of each forward to be first to the cross.

The crossing performance can be evaluated by counting the percentage of 'good' crosses (those providing a scoring opportunity) and 'bad' crosses (where the player could not get on the end of the pass). Shooting evaluation can be based on the ratio of crosses (only count those which allow an attempt on goal) to shots on target/goals.

SHOOTING ANALYSIS SCENARIO

This scenario provides a practical example of the match analysis process used to examine shooting performance.

Situation

An elite youth central defender has recently asked to play as a centre-forward. The player has great physical attributes and has scored several goals as a defender through outstanding heading ability. However, whilst the player immediately fits in well with general team play, the coach feels that the player's shooting is technically weak, because of several scoring opportunities having been missed.

Observation and analysis methods

Using a digital camcorder, the coach decides to film the centre-forward's performance over five matches in order to gain an overall picture of how well the player is performing. The coach is positioned next to the pitch to get close-in shots of the player. An assistant also notes the number of possible scoring opportunities and both on- and off-target shots. Finally, the coach prepares several clips of elite performers in action for comparison purposes.

Evaluation

First, the coach compiles the shooting statistics. From the data, it can be seen that the player missed 4 possible scoring chances through taking an extra touch on 3 occasions and that only 2 shots out of 10 were on target (20 per cent success rate) for 1 goal scored (with a header). Out of these 8 off-target shots, 6 were struck over the bar.

Using the digital film footage, the coach carefully analyses each shooting action using repeated viewing and slow-motion playback, and by freezing certain images. Specific aspects of technical performance such as the position of the non-kicking foot and head and the amount of power put into the shot are looked at in detail. On several occasions the coach notices that basic technical mistakes have been made. The coach also subjectively evaluates the player's body language by looking at factors such as confidence and composure.

Feedback

The coach speaks individually to the centre-forward and presents the statistical data. Detailed video feedback is provided using the playback techniques mentioned earlier. The coach asks the player to indicate where the probable mistakes are being made. Having pointed out and discussed the various problems in detail, the coach then shows examples of elite performance to demonstrate what the player must aim to achieve. The coach also mentions that over 75 per cent of goals in professional soccer are scored from one touch, in order to give an idea of the standard required at elite levels. The coach is careful to congratulate the player for actually getting into the shooting positions. Finally, the coach and player agree on extra sessions and aim at significantly increasing the percentage of shots on target.

Training

Over the next two weeks the player stays behind after training for extra shooting practice. The coach works on both the problematic areas mentioned: general shooting technique and one-touch finishing.

Organisation (shooting technique)

- Half pitch.
- Three servers, 1 shooting player, 1 goalkeeper.
- Large supply of balls and ball retrievers.

Description

Server 1 plays the ball in from behind the forward no. 9, who shoots at goal (Figure 8.4). After following the shot in, the player jogs back to his original starting position.

Server 2 plays the ball in horizontally from the right side and server 3 provides an angled pass from the left side. This sequence can be repeated ten to twenty times.

The servers aim to make the player use both feet.

Variations/progressions

- Add defenders to pressure the forward once the player's confidence and technique are satisfactory.
- Vary pass delivery (e.g. bouncing, volleys).
- Vary shooting distances and angles.
- Make the player sprint back to his/her original position to increase the physical intensity of the drill.

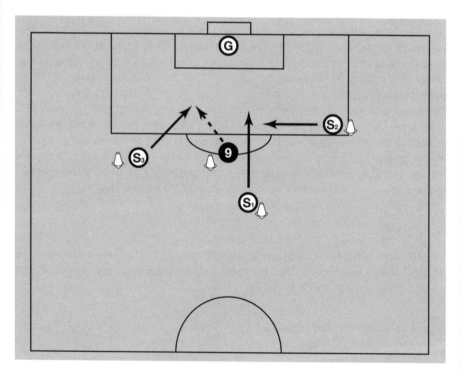

Figure 8.4 *Example of a simple training drill to improve general shooting technique*

Further analysis and evaluation

The coach has designed a simple drill to analyse shooting technique. The assessment can be based on the ability of the player to select the target area of the goal and to observe the goalkeeper's position, the accuracy and power of the shot, position of the head and non-kicking foot, and the kicking contact with the ball.

The session can easily be filmed to allow further analysis.

Performance can be evaluated by counting the ratio of on- to off-target shots or goals scored.

Organisation (one-touch finishing)

- Penalty area.
- Three servers outside penalty area, 3 forwards, 1 defender and 1 goalkeeper.
- Large supply of balls.

Description

This drill uses a conditioned game with limited ball touches to force players into taking rapid decisions such as analysing the time and space they have when shooting as well as practising general shooting technique. The ball is played from outside the box (Figure 8.5) by a server (alternate the service from each side of the box

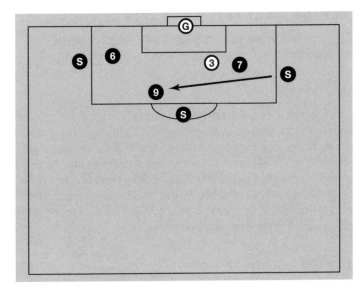

Figure 8.5 *Example of a training drill to improve one-touch finishing*

and from behind) to one of the forwards who has created space. The forwards are limited to two-touch passing, one-touch scoring and to three or fewer passes before a shot is taken. The other players should follow the shot in.

Variations/progressions

Add two more defenders (one by one) to reduce time, space and increase pressure once the forward's confidence and technique are satisfactory.

The forwards can play off the servers, who are free to move.

Further analysis and evaluation

General finishing techniques, instinct and choice of action in front of goal should be analysed. The coach should look at the player's ability to shoot as quickly as possible and to take the right option according to his/her position. The coach can also look at the off-the-ball movement to create space and body language for signs that the player is lacking confidence or decisiveness.

Evaluation can be through the number of goals scored or number of missed opportunities or balls lost.

GOALKEEPING ANALYSIS SCENARIO

This scenario provides a practical example of the match analysis process used to examine a goalkeeper's performance when dealing with crosses.

Situation

Over the last few matches the goalkeeper has made several errors when dealing with crosses, leading to two soft goals and various dangerous situations. The keeper is normally extremely reliable, but the player's form and confidence are stuttering after one previous mistake cost the team an important match. The defenders also seem to be suffering from a knock-on effect, as they seem less composed. perhaps as a result of having less confidence in the goalkeeper's capacities. The team manager asks the specialist goalkeeping coach to analyse the keeper's performance, evaluate the results and provide relevant feedback.

Observation and analysis methods

Although the club usually films and analyses every game, the goalkeeping coach decides to analyse in more detail the goalkeeper's performance using software which can be personalised to code any element of play. First, the coach codes every action involving the keeper using the advanced playback options to freeze the action and provide slow-motion playback. The coding involves classifying the different elements (e.g. starting position, flight assessment, decision-making, attacking the ball, catching or punching) involved in dealing with crosses as either correct or incorrect. A short edited video on the most relevant actions from each game is prepared. The coach analyses the last ten matches in order to have both positive (before the mistake) and negative (after the mistake) aspects of performance.

Evaluation

Having examined the performance in detail, the coach concludes that lack of confidence has led to basic errors creeping into the goalkeeper's game. The initial positioning in relation to the angle and distance of the ball is fine, but the goalkeeper seems indecisive when coming for the ball. In the last two matches the player has also started to punch rather than catch the ball. The statistics show a much greater ratio of *incorrect* to *correct* performance. For example, in the first five matches the keeper successfully played the ball (either caught or punched) from 80 per cent of the crosses compared to only 20 per cent in the last five matches. The coach talks to the team manager about the conclusions and they decide to speak to the keeper on an individual basis.

Feedback

Before undertaking any statistical or video-based analysis, the coach and manager take time to listen to the goalkeeper. The player explains that the costly mistake is preying on his/her mind and that he/she has lost confidence. Both try to encourage the keeper that through hard work on the training pitch, confidence will return. They then work through the edited video recording explaining step by step where the errors are occurring. Using the split-screen video option, they simultaneously show two images of contrasting match performance whilst insisting that the dip in form is only temporary. The goalkeeper agrees to go 'back to basics' and work on technique and judgement. The goalkeeping coach also decides to film the training sessions to evaluate progress and provide further feedback. They decide upon a set training plan over the next four days.

Training

Over the next week the goalkeeper spends time working individually with the reserve keeper. Each daily session aims at working on and gradually perfecting the basic skills required for dealing with crosses in order for the keeper to regain confidence and re-experience success, along with the ultimate aim of attaining and bettering his previous levels of performance.

Organisation

- Penalty area with two goals 18 yards apart.
- Two goalkeepers and two servers.
- Large supply of balls.

Description

This drill specifically aims at improving the keeper's confidence when dealing with crosses outside the 6-yard area (Figure 8.6). Server no. 1 randomly calls the name of the keeper to deal with the cross. The server only plays the ball into the space outside the 6-yard area. The crosses can be either in- or out-swinging.

The goalkeeper must take the decision to come for the ball. If the ball is caught by the keeper, it is thrown back to the same server.

The second server then repeats the drill.

Both keepers assess each other's performance.

'Easier' crosses may be played in at the beginning to build up confidence gradually.

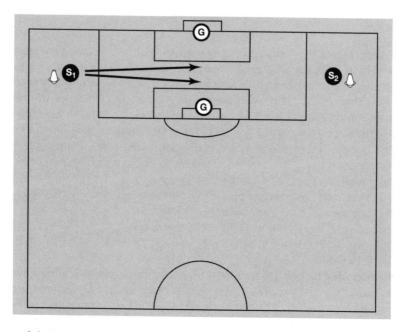

Figure 8.6 *Example of a training drill to improve the way a goalkeeper deals with crosses into the danger areas*

Variations/progressions

- Add passive attackers and active players to challenge for the cross and defenders to focus on communication.
- Vary the height and power of crosses (such as hard and low cutbacks).
- Sessions may also include crosses into the 6-yard box.
- The coach can create conditioned small-sided games to increase the number of crosses.

Further analysis and evaluation

Many different goalkeeping coaching points need to be assessed: starting position, stance, ball flight assessment, early decision-making, attacking the ball, handling technique and recovery lines. The goalkeeper will learn through the decisions made and the techniques employed in the session and their subsequent effect on performance.

The goalkeeper's performance can be evaluated through the number and/or percentage of correctly and incorrectly handled crosses.

SUMMARY

This chapter presents the different aspects of performance that can be analysed from a technical and tactical point of view as well as ideas on how this information can fit into tactical training. Having detailed information on match play is of little use if it cannot be practically translated by coaches into providing quality performance feedback and into designing and executing specific training sessions and drills. It is also important to provide further feedback from analysis and evaluation of performance during these training sessions to indicate individual and team progression.

CHAPTER NINE

▼ THE FUTURE OF SOCCER MATCH ANALYSIS

INTRODUCTION

It is human nature to strive constantly for improvements in what we do and how we do things on a daily basis. Soccer is no different, and many coaches are constantly looking for ways of enhancing performance. Throughout this book we have tried to demonstrate how and why match analysis can play an important part in improving performance. The match analysis process will undoubtedly be affected by current and future technological developments. Therefore, the aim of this chapter is to examine what may lie ahead in the future.

NEW METHODS OF OBTAINING DATA

The technology used to analyse player performance will no doubt continue to move forward in the way it already has done over the past few years. New and improved computer and video systems will be used in the collection, analysis and application of match data. Many companies involved in this field are constantly looking at ways of improving the collection of data in terms of speed, quality and quantity. These methods will no doubt include coding logics, voice recognition and global positioning systems (GPS).

Coding logic

Current coding methods involve the time-consuming and repetitive input of factors such as player names, actions and positions. As is mentioned in Chapter 4, voice recognition is one particular means of speeding up the coding of matches. The majority of systems will probably integrate voice recognition in some way. Systems will also no doubt use some form of special coding logic to save time when inputting data.

Consider a simple situation involving a pass between two players leading to an off-target shot. A *logic* could be used to reduce the amount of information to be coded. Figure 9.1 presents a schematic pitch representation of the match action. First, the analyst inputs the player's name (here: A) by voice recognition and clicks the position where the ball was received on the schematic pitch displayed in the computer interface (the time is automatically recorded, thanks to the time code). Voice recognition is again used to input the other player's name (here: B) and the position clicked on the pitch. As the ball is transferred from one player (here A to B) to another in the same team, the computer recognises this as a successful pass (the two positions also provide information on pass direction and length). The process of simply clicking two different positions and inputting two names by voice recognition avoids having to look for and click on the pass button in the interface. The analyst then clicks a further position where B touched the ball again and then input a shot by voice recognition. The ball position is clicked (the shot went wide) behind the goal line. As B kept possession, there is no point in inputting the player's name

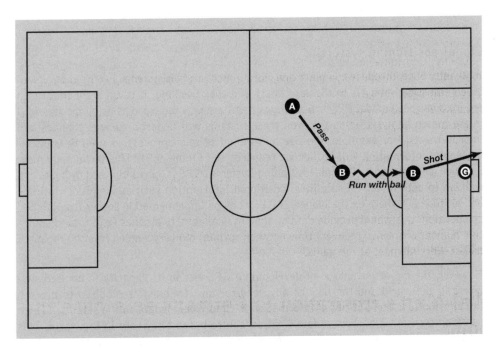

Figure 9.1 *In the future the coding of a simple match action such as a pass, run with the ball and shot will be made easier through the use of a coding logic and voice recognition*

again, therefore saving another click (two different positions also mean a run with the ball). Also, clicking the position behind the goal where the ball went wide means that the computer automatically recognises that the shot was unsuccessful. Finally, as the ball goes behind for what obviously had to be a goal kick, the computer automatically calculates from the position of the last click that the next action must be a goal kick, so avoiding the input of yet another match action. Although sufficient practice is needed to learn such coding strategies, the time required to analyse a match could be drastically reduced, especially when combined with voice recognition.

Other data collection methods

Finger touch-sensitive screens will be employed by some systems, and new optical technology developed to record positions of actions on the interface pitch through measuring where the eye is looking. These methods will gradually phase out the use of the mouse and keyboard. Systems will also allow several operators to work simultaneously on the same match, recording through a local network or over the Internet. The more quickly the system can produce the required results, the more attractive it is to coaches.

The ultimate aim for future systems is the development and application of intelligent technology to analyse match performance without any human input. Using sophisticated player and ball tracking methods, digital video and sound, these systems will automatically recognise and record every action and movement as it happens on the pitch. Such a system is a few years away from being developed, but rapid technological developments may allow this type of system to see the light of day within the next decade or two.

Global positioning systems

In Chapter 3 we introduce computer and video match analysis systems. From simple video-based statistical analysis to the very latest in player tracking, it is apparent that much progress has been made. Player tracking systems are now regarded as being the standard in the match analysis field. Yet even these systems will undergo various changes and improvements. For example, the size and weight of microprocessors used to transmit movement information will be further reduced (see Figure 9.2). This technology may, however, be replaced by Global Positioning Systems (GPSs), currently used by boats and walkers to determine, via satellites, positional information such as longitude, latitude and altitude anywhere on the planet. If GPSs can be implemented in soccer training and competition, this would provide data on the physical activity profiles (e.g. total distance run, number of sprints, recovery time between sprints) of every single player on the pitch and at every moment of the game.

However, the major advantage of developing a GPS lies in its capacity to be used anywhere in the world and the lack of any need for on-site logistics required to process the information. The positional information is simply beamed up to the satellite, which can then transfer it back to a data analysis centre based elsewhere in the world. This means that in contrast to video-based or microprocessor tracking, performance in away matches can easily be analysed. Nevertheless, there are several major disadvantages with using GPSs:

Figure 9.2 *Example of the size, compared to a small coin, of a microchip tag developed and used by the German technology company Cairos. These chips are small enough to be hidden easily in shin pads, boots or even shirts*

- Players must carry the tracking device, which is currently forbidden by FIFA.
- Current systems demonstrate a lack of portability, owing to the fact that the devices are relatively heavy and bulky, hence they cannot be worn by players during matches or training. However, by the time this book is published, given the current rapid advances in technology, the latest GPS may be the size of a postage stamp.
- The device requires the use of batteries, which can run out quickly and may not stand up to severe shocks.
- Such systems may not function correctly in soccer stadia and are often influenced by temperature and land configuration.
- GPSs are still relatively expensive. The more expensive versions are lighter, smaller and more accurate.
- Analysis is often restricted to one positional measurement per second. This means that these devices are limited in analysing accelerations, decelerations and changes in direction.

In the future, this type of tracking data could be linked to the data produced by devices measuring physiological information such as heart rate to provide an excellent picture of the overall player effort. GPSs will also be developed to transmit this type of data.

The Internet

The Internet will play a similarly important role in the future of match analysis. The incredible development over recent years of this computer network allows much more flexibility in the way match analysis data are collected, transferred and made available for viewing. As mentioned earlier, the coding of matches will be possible from anywhere in the world as a result of faster connection speeds (broadband), allowing match analysts to work in real time on a game recording transferred over the Internet. This will drastically reduce the cost of transporting staff and equipment.

As the matches will be coded live, the data will be processed in real time and sent back for immediate analysis and evaluation by the coaching team. This can easily be done via email. Many modern systems provide an output function to publish data automatically (such as video sequences or graphs) into Web format for future retrieval. These data can also be displayed on a Web site address for usage by any coach or player, anywhere in the world. Recent faster connection speed has made this transfer process even easier. Post-match, the coach may want to organise a live Web-based video conference to discuss the performance with staff members back home.

It is also important to mention that the World Wide Web is also a fantastic means for sharing information and ideas. Many coaches are now using forums, Web sites and live chats to search for and share new ideas. Web sites containing databases of training drills and articles on fitness and tactical issues are now commonplace, although quality of content vary markedly. However, any coach should be aware of the wealth of free information currently available on the Web twenty-four hours a day.

DATA AND RESULTS

Future improvements also concern the way the results from match analysis are processed and used. Digital video technology will continue to make progress in terms of quality and price. One of the current limitations of digital video is the large amount of computer storage space required. The larger the video screen size recording and the higher the quality, the greater the hard disk/CD/DVD-ROM space required. Currently, a DVD-ROM often only contains one match recording, and even this has often undergone compression to reduce file size and therefore quality. Coaches may currently see digital video footage as being less desirable than its traditional analogue counterpart, because of the poorer image quality and size. Future digital video techniques will allow large-screen and extremely high-quality footage to be comfortably stored on disk format, thanks to improved non-degrading compression techniques. Furthermore, the cameras used to record the footage will provide easier and better-quality recordings thanks to intelligent automatic image adjustment, which will avoid or reduce problems such as light exposure.

Currently, tracking systems allow a reconstruction in two dimensions of the positions, movements and actions of every player on the pitch at every moment of the game. Using the same data, this work has recently been extended to three-dimensional reconstructions using player representations (see Figure 9.3). However, both two- and three-dimensional analysis are restricted, as they do not show any real behavioural or technical information, unlike a video recording. For example, the two-dimensional analysis may show that when the goal was conceded, a player's marking and position were correct. However, match video might show that the player was seemingly watching the ball and was therefore caught out by the forward. Therefore, an ideal futuristic system would combine tracking data with an exact reconstruction of player postural information such as which way the player was facing and looking, and his/her body positions as well as technical skills such as how and where the ball was struck. The Soccerman project developed by the Institute of Computer Science and Applied Mathematics based at the University of Bern is a first step in this direction. This type of system would allow for the first time the analysis and evaluation of every aspect of performance.

Expert systems (an application that uses a knowledge base of human expertise to aid in solving problems) using artificial intelligence (which is the branch of computer science

Figure 9.3 *A match reconstruction in three dimensions created by the Israeli sports technology company ORAD*

concerned with making computers behave like humans) will probably start to play a major role in the modelling and prediction of performance. Expert systems will be designed to analyse and understand match performance and develop the most efficient and optimal training sessions. For example, the expert system computer will advise on how performance can be improved by delivering information on areas such as fitness, and will design tailor-made training schedules. This will be possible as these systems will combine qualitative and quantitative information derived from the knowledge and expertise of coaches and technical staff (e.g. fitness trainer, defensive coach) and from data obtained through training sessions and matches. The system will then measure the progress made in both matches and training, answer coach and player questions, supply explanations on performance-related issues and apply or suggest ways of improving the training model.

These expert systems may also play a part in helping coaches to analyse live performance. For example, a system can be programmed to provide intelligent information on performance (using both past and current information) and make decisions which are then practically translated into coaching terms. The following analysis offers a glance into what may lie ahead.

EXPERT SYSTEM SCENARIO

This scenario provides a practical example of how an expert system could be used by coaches.

The coach uses the expert system to help prepare for the match. The system exploits a database containing both quantitative and qualitative information on the opposition tactics (e.g. tend to pressure high up the field, direct game), playing system (e.g. 4-4-2 with zonal marking), technique (e.g. the preferred foot of individual players) as well as work-rate data (e.g. fastest player and who runs the most). The expert system then offers a model containing practical advice on how to optimise both team and player defence and attack. The coach will then take this into account and use the information acquired in training to prepare players both individually and collectively for the match. The system will also take into account the team's previous matches against this team to provide examples of unsuccessful and successful performance and suggest how and what must be done to win.

During the game, the expert system will automatically provide alerts on instances of good performance or ongoing problems. For example, the centre-forward has only touched the ball twice in the last 10 minutes and has only made five sprints, and the last two were shorter and slower than normal; the midfield players have had a low share of ball possession and have won few duels; the defence is positioned too far back compared to previous matches and the distance between the right-back and the opposing winger is increasing. The expert system will then query the database to provide examples of games with examples of similarly negative performance and attempt to provide real-time solutions to the problem (e.g. substitutions, change of tactics). It will also try to build on the positive play and offer further solutions and advice on how to take advantage of the opposition's weaknesses.

In this match the team managed a replay, perhaps in part thanks to the expert system, which will then provide a post-match summary on what when wrong as well as an appropriate training programme to improve specific aspects of play. For example, the centre-forward will be given a personalised training programme to work on sprint endurance in order to improve his/her capacity to repeat high-intensity efforts. Finally, the expert system will attempt to predict the outcome of the replay by taking into account these changes and improvements.

NEW TRAINING METHODS

Coaches at all levels face the difficult task of creating challenging lesson plans for their team on a regular basis. They are often on the lookout for new ideas to improve performance through innovative training methods. One particular means of improving player learning is by aiding players' understanding of the tasks they must carry out. Indeed, clear and precise instructions are an important component of any learning process. For many years, soccer coaches have used 'traditional' methods to design and present training drills and tactics to players. The blackboard and chalk is a popular method, as are magnetic tactic boards where the players are represented by draughts on a pitch. Some coaches even continue to use simple pen-and-paper drawings. However, these methods are known to have various disadvantages:

- Static presentations do not represent the true nature of soccer play.
- Players can find it difficult to understand the timing of the movements and actions to be carried out in the drill.
- The drawings are often untidy and difficult to read and understand.
- There is no efficient way of archiving and reusing each drill, hence time is lost recreating or retrieving the same drills.

One of the reasons that coaches continue to use older-style methods is a lack of familiarity with and hence dislike of modern technology. This is unfortunate, as multimedia offer new and exciting chances for learning, and computer animations help bring a new dimension to the game. In order to improve on this conventional way of working, various technology companies have designed and created software to animate and bring to life these Xs and Os. Animation packages are now used by coaches at all levels of the game to recreate and display training drills manually as well as demonstrate the general principles of attacking and defensive organisation. In addition, specific tactical and, to a certain extent, technical errors made during match play can also be recreated and analysed. Through enhanced awareness of movement patterns and a clearer understanding of game strategies, players' performances can be improved.

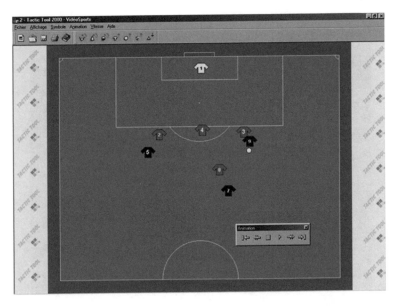

Figure 9.4 *Example of a commercial software interface (Tactic Tool by Sport-Universal Process). The animation control bar (bottom right of the screen) allows easy playback of a 3 versus 4 attacking drill. The overhead viewing perspective provides a clear view of players' positions, movements and actions (courtesy of Sport-Universal Process)*

This technological approach was also used by the French Football Federation to assess the various strategies and playing patterns of opponents during its preparations for the 1998 World Cup. Using a laptop connected to a video projector, the federation's match analyst presented the opposition's tactics and playing system using manually created tactical animations linked to a digital video recording. For example, opposition set plays such as corners and free kicks were closely analysed and a detailed breakdown of each type of action was presented to the French players. This method is still used by the French Football Federation, and a huge library of defensive and attacking information on many national teams has been created. UEFA also used the TACTFOOT animation software (Figure 9.5) during Euro 2004 to analyse tactically each team's performances, and the same software is used in England by all the Football Association's national squads.

Although computerised simulations are not a direct component of match analysis, they play a complementary part in the preparation, analysis and evaluation of training and match play. Defining, coaching and improving team strategy and tactics are of paramount importance in soccer. Simulation software can help draw up and bring to life player movements, positions and actions for various game and training elements such as playing systems, set plays, attacking and build-up play, defending play and fitness drills and tests. The advantages of this type of software are as follows:

- Players can actually visualise the required positions, movements and actions in drills. Soccer is a game whose characteristics include movement, timing and speed of actions. Animations allow the coach to show where the players should be positioned, where they should be running and where the ball should be passed.

Figure 9.5 *Some packages allow drills to be presented from different viewing perspectives. The TACTFOOT software (AVC Media Enterprises Ltd) demonstrates the positions and marking of players in a corner drill from an innovative three-dimensional viewing angle*

- The drills can be repeatedly played back at different speeds for better understanding and paused during discussions, e.g. in pre-match or training team talks.
- Each individual drill can be stored on a computer and easily reused whenever desired. Depending on the software, these drills can be printed off to obtain a hard copy and used in overhead presentations. They may even be exchanged between coaches through the Internet to facilitate the sharing of ideas and tactics and training drills developed and learnt through personal experience.
- Laptops and especially handheld devices with a database of stored drills may be brought onto the training area for use by the coach. This type of equipment, like basic desktop computers, is now relatively affordable.
- These drills may be combined with video footage to complement animations and projected onto a large screen during team talks and presentations.
- The drills can be fun and become an interesting learning tool for younger players. The French sports software company Sport-Universal Process has developed animation software which provides various questions and quizzes on different aspects of match play and the rules of the game. For example, the learner has to visualise several animated examples of an offside situation to help understand match play and rules. Each individual offensive action must be analysed and the correct answer selected where the attacking player is actually offside as a result of player movements and positions. Another example commonly used is the presentation of the roles of individual players such as a right-back or centre-forward. The learner can see descriptions and various animated examples of common match situations involving these players. Knowledge can also be gained on how to deal correctly with these situations.
- Animated drills can also help ease the integration of new players into the team's existing tactics and strategy through easier and quicker understanding.

It is always important, however, to underline the various disadvantages of any modern technology used in the coaching and education of soccer players. For example, probably the major stumbling block encountered by coaches is the time required to build up a database of tactics. Even though individual tactics are relatively quick to create, thanks to user-friendly software, reproducing a lifetime's content of drills will take time and energy. The other factor which may also discourage coaches is a lack of experience or skills in information technology. In addition, players may be unaccustomed to this type of presentation and could initially be confused. Finally, whilst systems are relatively cheap, the overall investment required (computer, printer, and so on) may be too great for some coaches.

Another area currently looked at in various research projects around the world is the effectiveness of simulated Internet-enhanced instruction compared to traditional on-the-pitch instruction. Players may log on to the Internet and see graphical and video examples of their own tactical and technical performance compared to expert models. The players can view the actions from any angle or a number of different angles and at different speeds. This approach may be useful in helping them to see the skills they were supposed to be trying to perform and can give them something to focus on during training.

This type of information may also be useful when attempting to develop anticipation or decision-making skill. Skilled soccer players develop, through practice and instruction, an extensive database of the likely scenarios and situations that will arise during a match. This knowledge of the likely probabilities of certain events occurring is important in guiding players' search for information and helps them to anticipate situations before they arise. Players could therefore access specific situational probabilities stored on computer about the likely outcomes to expect when playing against any team (e.g. highest probability that the fullback in possession of the ball in a certain situation will make this type of pass) or when facing a particular opponent (e.g. player X always cuts onto his left foot in a certain situation or player Y has a tendency to make a certain type of run into the penalty area). Such information would ensure that players were 'cued in' to important information and would greatly facilitate game-reading skills.

Taking this approach even further is the use of virtual reality, which may be defined as the simulation of a real or imagined environment that can be experienced visually in three dimensions with sound, tactile and other forms of feedback. This approach has previously been used in other sports (such as bobsleigh and American football) as a training mechanism by simulating the environment of elite competition through the use of material such as cyber eyeglasses, data-generating gloves and simulators. This environment will allow players to experience and relive all the sensations (e.g. crowd noises, wind, rain) they usually feel in real competition as well as providing visual and motion cues on performance. Virtual reality aims to speed up learning time and the achievement of optimal performance. The system will also use relevant information on all aspects of playing performance such as fitness and tactics to maximise the effect. For example, a goalkeeper could play in a virtual soccer match simulator. The player sees, experiences and participates in the game from a first-person perspective. The computer can recreate match actions such as penalty kicks or crosses. The goalkeeper's performance can then be analysed during each particular action and virtual reality then used to work on and improve specific techniques. Players wearing a computer-linked virtual reality suit will be helped and guided through the exact movements required, again using an expert model. For example, a player who is struggling to strike the ball properly could be aided as the computer will 'guide' the player through the movement by detecting errors and correcting factors such as the position of feet and head and where the ball should be struck.

The virtual reality system can be used to train goalkeepers to anticipate the direction of a penalty taker's shot. Such an approach has already been used in cricket and tennis, and a similar system has been developed to train decision-making skill in American football (see http://www-VRL.umich.edu/project/football). This virtual reality approach is also useful for players who are injured or recovering; it means that they can practise in a contact-free environment. On the downside, one side effect players may experience when immerged in a virtual environment is a feeling of cybersickness (a form of motion sickness where disorientation, disequilibrium and nausea can occur). To reduce the risk of cybersickness, players may require an initial adaptation period, shorter exposure time and the restriction of demanding gross motor movements.

PLAYER DETECTION, TRANSFERS AND PERFORMANCE-RELATED PAY

Talent-spotting methods and player transfers are often the subject of much speculation in the modern era. Whatever the age group, the top players are regularly offered astronomic sums to either stay or move on to a different club. But on what criteria are these transfers based? A centre-forward may be judged on the number of goals scored and, conversely, a goalkeeper on the number of goals conceded.

Detailed match statistics may have an important role to play in future discussions between players and clubs. After the usual medical assessments, a club hesitating between two 'top' midfielders may desire a detailed breakdown of the match performances of each player over the previous season. Data show that in terms of tactical and technical performance (e.g. passing shooting, tackling), both are similar. However, work-rate data show that the first player generally covers more ground and is less subject to a drop-off in workload towards the end of games. Furthermore, physiological profiling shows a significant difference in maximal aerobic power. Therefore, the club may lean towards this player. The same player could also use this type of data to increase personal demands.

In recent years, the serious financial problems endured by clubs are due in part to the enormous salaries earned by players. One method to reduce this deficit could be to introduce performance-related pay, a method currently employed by many companies in traditional industries. Match analysis may be useful in terms of designating who earns what! A centre-forward scoring 30 goals a season would, it seems, be relatively easy to reward. On the other hand, how could output of a midfield player be quantified? His/her salary could be partly based on the number and success rate of various match actions such as tackles, passes, goal assists, clearances or on work-rate data such as the number of sprints or the total distance covered. The criteria for calculating performance-related pay in soccer have yet to be defined. Nevertheless, match data may have a small part to play.

DRUG DETECTION

Drugs affect the physiology and performance of players. Laboratory-controlled measurements are generally used to test for improvements in performance by examining physiological factors such as heart rate, oxygen uptake, lactate levels, muscle strength or power. In soccer, drugs aim at improving aerobic and anaerobic capacity. However, could match analysis data play a role in detecting drug abuse by measuring improvements in actual match performance? The performance of a sprinter who dramatically reduced the world 100-metre record by 0.2 seconds would no doubt be closely scrutinised, so why not that of soccer players?

In studies on athletes, various substances including creatine, which is not banned, have been shown to improve sprint times and the ability to recover in a shorter period of time. A detailed work-rate profile of a centre-forward's high-intensity actions may indicate that the player's maximal sprinting speed has increased and he/she sprints more often and spends less time in recovery activities. When compared to previous analyses of the same player, this indicates a significant gain in physical performance and may warrant further investigation.

Similarly, erythropoietin (EPO) has been shown to increase maximum aerobic power. This drug may have implications, as $V_{O_2\ max}$ is significantly correlated to the distances run by soccer players. A midfielder who regularly ran around 10 km during a match is suddenly achieving distances of around 11 km, amounting to a gain of around 10 per cent. Neither the tactical role of the player nor the team's playing system has been changed. As the endurance capacity of soccer players is highly linked to work-rate performance, this may once again imply the use of drugs. Professional soccer has up to now steered relatively clear of doping, with only a few reported cases. However, match analysis and in particular work-rate profiles may in theory play a small yet important role in helping detect drug infringements.

SUMMARY

This chapter has presented various future technological developments in the field of match analysis. Some of the technology mentioned may well be in use by the time this book goes to press. However, whilst technology is constantly improving, coaches need to be aware of how they can use and make the most of these new methods to analyse performance. This requires a good technological background along with an open mind, particularly for coaches at elite levels, who now need to be at the forefront of technology.

▼ FURTHER READING

If you are interested in reading more about soccer match analysis or match analysis in general, there are several books entirely dedicated to the topic (1–3, 9), providing various chapters of interest (7) or presenting conference proceedings collating specific research (4–6, 8, 10). The coaching journal *Insight* published twice a year by the English Football Association, is another useful resource for match analysis.

1 Bertuzzi, G. (1999) *Soccer Scouting Guide Book*, Reedswain, Spring City, Pennsylvania.
2 Hughes, M. D. and Franks, I. M. (eds) (2004) *Notational Analysis of Sport: Systems for Better Coaching and Performance*, E. & F. N. Spon, London.
3 Kormelink, H. and Seeveren, T. (1999) *Match Analysis and Game Preparation Book*, Reedswain, Spring City, Pennsylvania.
4 Reilly, T., Lees, A., Davids, K. and Murphy, W. (1988) *Science and Football*, E. & F. N. Spon, London.
5 Reilly, T., Stibbe, A. and Clarys, J. (1993) *Science and Football II*, E. & F. N. Spon, London.
6 Reilly, T., Bangsbo, J. and Hughes, M. (1997) *Science and Football III*, E. & F. N. Spon, London.
7 Reilly, T. and Williams, A. M. (eds) (2003) *Science and Soccer II*, E. & F. N. Spon, London.
8 Reilly, T., Cabri, J. and Aranjo, D. (ed.) (2005) *Science and Football V*, Routledge, London.
9 Robertson, K. (2002) *Observation, Analysis and Video*, National Coaching Foundation, Leeds.
10 Spinks, W., Reilly, T. and Murphy, A. (eds) (2002) *Science and Football IV*, Routledge , London.

▼ INDEX

HANDBOOK OF SOCCER MATCH ANALYSIS

LEARNING

FA COACHES ASSOCIATION (FACA)
SETTING THE STANDARD IN FOOTBALL COACHING

The FA has put FACA members on course to become the gold standard of coaching. Not only will all FACA members be qualified coaches and up to date on all the latest developments, but their Criminal Records Bureau (CRB) checks will ensure the coaches are accepted at clubs and centres throughout the country.

This is excellent news for coaches because increasingly schools, local authorities, professional clubs and clubs affiliated to football in England, will only accept trained and qualified people with the most up to date credentials.

The FA is determined to offer the best possible value for money to FACA members. To achieve this aim we have designed an attractive benefit package that is detailed below.

Membership Benefits

• **An Initial Joining Pack Consisting of:**
FACA Membership Card depending upon membership status.
Civil Liability Insurance Certificate for Licenced Coaches resident in the UK.

• **Exclusive "Insight" Journal**
Two issues per year of "Insight" - The official half yearly Journal of FACA.

• **Free Access to Insight Live**
The official online coaching resource for FACA members providing 24 hour access.

• **£5m Civil Liability Insurance Protection for Licenced Coaches**

• **Personal Accident Insurance Protection for Licenced Coaches**

• **Exclusive Education and Training Opportunities**
FACA members will have the opportunity to enrol upon a programme of National Courses, Conferences and Conventions, some of which are exclusive to Licenced Coaches.

• **Coaching Merchandise**
Licenced Coaches will be able to purchase exclusive FACA branded merchandise.

• **FACA Resource Catalogue**
The FACA Resource Catalogue, including carefully selected resources,
dedicated to providing an important service to coaches.

• **FA CRB Enhanced Disclosure**
The FA takes the welfare of children seriously and has introduced a comprehensive FA CRB checking process. Successful completion of this process is required to be become a member of FACA.

Any queries about the process must be directed to The FA CRB Unit at **CRB@TheFA.com** and not to FACA.

To download your FACA forms please go to **www.TheFA.com/FALearning** or alternatively call the FALearning Hotline on **0870 8500 424**.